The

Boethian Commentaries

of

Clarembald of Arras

Notre Dame Texts in Medieval Culture

VOL. 7

Medieval Institute

University of Notre Dame

The

Boethian Commentaries

of

Clarembald of Arras

Translated by

DAVID B. GEORGE

and

JOHN R. FORTIN, O.S.B.

University of Notre Dame Press • Notre Dame, Indiana

Manufactured in the United States of America

Library of Congress Cataloging-in-Publication Data
Clarembald, of Arras, 12th cent.
[Tractatus super librum Boetii De Trinitate. English]
The Boethian commentaries of Clarembald of Arras / translated and
edited by David B. George and John R. Fortin.
p. cm. — (Notre Dame texts in medieval culture ; v. 7)
ISBN 0-268-02168-6 (cloth : alk. paper)
1. Boethius, d. 524. De Trinitate.   2. Trinity—Early works to
1800.   3. Boethius, d. 524. Quomodo substantiae.   4. Substance
(Philosophy)—Moral and ethical aspects—Early works to 1800.
I. George, David B., 1950– . II. Fortin, John R., 1949– .
III. Clarembald, of Arras, 12th cent. Expositio super librum Boetii
De hebdomadibus. English.   IV. Title.   V. Series.
BT111.3.B643C53 2002
231'.044—dc21
2002009383

∞ *This is book is printed on acid-free paper.*

To
our families

Contents

We wish to acknowledge Reverend Finbar P. O'Mahoney, O.S.B.,
monk of Saint Anselm Abbey, Manchester, New Hampshire, and
professor emeritus of Classical Languages of Saint Anselm College,
for his invaluable assistance with an initial draft of this translation.

Ut in omnibus glorifectur Deus.
(*Rule of Saint Benedict* 57.9)

Translators' Introduction

To the student of medieval philosophy Clarembald of Arras is not always a familiar name or, if recognized at all, is not regarded as a significant figure in the intellectual life of the twelfth century. Indeed many histories of philosophy, if they mention Clarembald at all, uncritically categorize him as a typical example of the famous school at Chartres and a somewhat uninspired conveyor of the thought of the more renowned masters of his age under whom he studied. Although he served during his lifetime in various official positions, as a provost, an archdeacon, a chaplain, and a schoolmaster, he certainly fell under the influence of greater lights, especially his teachers Thierry of Chartres and Hugh of Saint Victor. Indeed in his writings he may appear to be a rather relentless disciple of his acknowledged masters: not only does he readily admit his dependence on them, he has only written on subjects on which works by Thierry already existed and from which he borrowed (or, in the view of one historian, plagiarized[1]).

Despite this prevailing view, however, there are two immediate facts that warrant a more careful examination of Clarembald's writing and thought, which would result in a nuancing of his position in the history of philosophy. The first is that his skills as an academician were so regarded by the then bishop of Laon, Walter of Mortagne, that he summoned Clarembald to his see city to assume the position of master of the school there. This school had earned much notoriety under the scholarly direction of the brothers Anselm and Ralph of Laon during the early years of the twelfth century. Even though the school was on the wane at the time of Clarembald's appointment, unable as it was to compete with the Paris schools, nonetheless one can assume that such an academically oriented bishop as Walter would have sought someone of tested competence to oversee an institution important at least within his own diocese. Thus Clarembald's appointment, even though for a short term, is an indication that his skills as an administrator and as a academician were recognized and appreciated.

The second fact is that Clarembald's reputation as a master of the thought of Boethius and his ability to clarify the confusions in the doctrinally suspect glosses of the bishop Gilbert of Poitiers moved certain religious in Laon (and possibly elsewhere) to request from Clarembald a gloss on Boethius's *De Trinitate*. This is important because what these people sought was not a copy of an extant work by Clarembald's renowned master Thierry of Chartres on that same Boethian *opusculum*. Rather they sought one of Clarembald's own composition which would address their specific concerns, namely their difficulties with the content and style of the bishop of Poitiers's gloss. Such a project was not envisioned by Thierry, and his gloss apparently would not have satisfied these readers. Clarembald acquiesced to their demands and produced not only a gloss on the *De Trinitate* but a subsequent gloss on another Boethian treatise, *De Hebdomadibus*.

Thus it would seem reasonable that a more accurate assessment than has heretofore been given of Clarembald's position in the intellectual history of the Middle Ages and in the tradition of commentaries on the theological treatises of Boethius would result from a closer study of his writings. These translations of Clarembald's glosses on Boethius's *De Trinitate* and *De Hebdomadibus* are intended to assist in that effort.

A Biography of Clarembald

The life of Clarembald received a most thorough treatment in Nikolaus M. Häring's critical edition of Clarembald's writings.[2] The Clarembald who is thought to have authored the glosses under consideration here first appears in the church records of Arras in 1152, wherein he is named *praepositus* or academic provost; he is in fact the sixth provost of Arras.[3] Four years later in 1156 Clarembald was raised to the office of archdeacon of that city under Bishop Godescalc. He continued to retain that position throughout the episcopacy of Godescalc's successor, Andrew of Paris. In 1174, upon the completion of the reign of Andrew, however, it was not Clarembald but another archdeacon, Frombald, who was elevated to the bishopric of Arras. From that time on Clarembald's name no longer appears in the Arras church records.

o him? Where did he go? A "Clarembald" makes a sud-
e records of the see of Laon in 1173 when he is named
s of the Church of Sts. Nicolas and James by Walter of
Laon (1152–1174). Walter's successor, Roger de Rozoy
(1174–1201), maintained Clarembald in that position at least through 1187,
after which time Clarembald's name ceases to appear in any official ecclesiastical documents of Laon.

It cannot be proved with certitude that the church records of Arras and
Laon refer to the same person. Nonetheless Clarembald's "retirement" to
Laon, after a career of twenty-two years in the ecclesiastical administration
of the see of Arras, does admit of the following tenuous explanation. According to a letter addressed to his friend Odo which was attached to one
of the manuscripts of his *DTr* (MS Saint-Omer, 192), Clarembald states that
he had at one time been the schoolmaster in Laon.[4] Careful scrutiny of the
records indicates when this situation might have occurred. Between 1152
and 1173 Clarembald's name is absent from the records in Arras for two brief
periods: 1157–1159 and 1165–1167. During both absences, it should be noted,
Walter was bishop in Laon. Angotus, the master of the school in Laon during
most of Walter's tenure, is absent from the church records there during 1158.
It is therefore possible, though not certain, that it was during the period
1157–1159 that Clarembald went to Laon at the request of Walter to serve as
"acting master" of the school during Angotus's absence. This brief appointment to the school, at whatever date, not only presents us with testimony of
Clarembald's recognized academic competence, this association between
Walter and Clarembald can help to explain a later appointment of Clarembald to a chaplaincy in Laon after he quit the archdiaconate of Arras.

One interesting historical reference to Clarembald is found in a biog-
raphy of Thomas Becket by a monk of Canterbury. This work contains a reference to Clarembald, archdeacon of Arras, who gave some relics of Becket
as a donation to a convent in Bapaume, a town about fifteen miles from
Arras.[5] Given that Becket was murdered on December 29, 1170, it may
be presumed that the donation occurred no sooner than a year or two later,
thus placing the donation around 1172–1173. Clarembald may have known
Thomas Becket as a student in Paris, for they were students there at the
same time. Further it is most interesting to note that Becket stayed in Arras
during part of his exile in 1164 at the time of Clarembald's tenure as archdeacon.[6]

Except for some scattered remarks in his writings, the above sketch of
Clarembald's professional life is all that can be affirmed with any degree of

certainty. In regard to his early life, Clarembald only tells us of a part of his formal education, namely that he studied the theological works of Boethius under the direction of Thierry of Chartres (d. 1155) and Hugh of St. Victor (d. 1142).[7] His education then most likely took place in Paris at a time when such personages as Thomas Becket and John of Salisbury were students, and when Peter Abelard and Gilbert of Poitiers were conducting classes.

Under the direction of Thierry and Hugh, Clarembald would have encountered the basic texts of the seven liberal arts, the trivium and quadrivium, and expositions thereof. If the educational programs of his two masters as found in their respective pedagogical works, *Heptateuchon*[8] and *Didascalicon,*[9] are any indication of the depth and thoroughness of their own interests and study, then the student Clarembald was most certainly exposed to one of the finest educational opportunities of his time. What advantage he took of these can be traced in part to and judged on the basis of his own writings.

Other lacunae in the life of Clarembald cannot be determined. There is no information about the time and place of his birth or his family background. It cannot be resolved whether Clarembald was a student right up to the time of his appointment to the office of provost in Arras in 1152, or whether he was a schoolmaster in Arras or elsewhere before that appointment, or perhaps even held some other position before entering ecclesiastical service. The place and time of his death are likewise unknown.

The Writings of Clarembald

There are three works attributed to Clarembald of Arras and they are found in five manuscripts. The first is a gloss on Boethius's *De Trinitate,* one of the two Boethian theological treatises which attempt to explain the mystery of three persons in one substance in the Godhead. This gloss is found in three manuscripts: MS Oxford, Balliol Coll. 296; MS Valenciennes, Bibl. mun. 193; MS Saint-Omer 142 (it is this latter manuscript which contains the biographically crucial and informative letter to Odo at the beginning of the gloss). The second work is a gloss on another Boethian theological treatise commonly known as *De Hebdomadibus* which investigates how it is that created things can be called good even though they are not substantially good. This is found in only one manuscript and accompanies one of the *De Trinitate* glosses: MS Saint-Omer 142. Finally there is a commentary on the six days of creation of Genesis 1 in imitation of the physical explanation of creation given in an accompanying text by Thierry of Chartres. This is found in two manuscripts: MS Paris, B.N. *Lat.* 3584 and MS Cambrai, Bibl. mun. 339.

The exact dating of the composition of these glosses is not certain. Clearly the Boethian glosses were composed during or after Clarembald's stay in Laon, as the prefatory letter to Odo indicates.[10] The *De Hebdomadibus* gloss refers several times to the previously published *De Trinitate* gloss and thus must have been composed sometime after it.[11] These glosses then can be situated at the earliest in the late 1150s. If the hexameron commentary was addressed to Queen Matilde,[12] then the *terminus ad quem* for its composition would be sometime in 1164, the time of Becket's exile and also of Matilde's death. Thus it would seem that Clarembald's scholarly writing activity is limited to a period from the late 1150s to the middle of the 1160s.

The writings of Boethius were no strangers to the medieval curriculum. Boethius (480–524) was a statesman and scholar of the late Roman period. Although he rose to the rank of consul under the emperor Theodoric, his efforts on behalf of the Senate eventually brought him into disfavor. He was imprisoned and sentenced to death. It was during this incarceration before his execution that he composed his famous *De consolatione philosophiae*, a significant source of Neoplatonic doctrine during the Middle Ages.

Besides his role as a statesman, Boethius had a lively intellectual life and was highly regarded in academic circles. His principal goal was to translate from Greek into Latin all the works of Plato and Aristotle, and by means of commentaries on them to show their compatibility. This tremendous project was cut short by his untimely death. He did nevertheless succeed, among other learned endeavors, in translating and commenting upon several of the logical works of Aristotle, in composing treatises on some of the liberal arts (his *De Musica,* for example, was the standard text for centuries), and in writing five theological treatises, the *Opuscula Sacra,* which were important texts in the medieval schools and concerning two of which Clarembald offered his own complete glosses.

The treatise commonly referred to as the *De Trinitate* has as its fuller title *Quomodo trinitas unus deus ac non tres dii.*[13] In it Boethius tries to explain the mystery of the "one God in three persons" definition which was put forth by the Council of Nicea against the Arians. Boethius leads his readers through his discussion by asserting clearly that the solution to this controversial question must be based upon an attempt to understand the nature of the Deity as it is in itself and not to explain it by means of natural analogies which can result in error. Boethius's explanation is grounded in two principles. The first is that not every instance of counting results in a multi-plicity. The second is that the proper application of the predicate "relation" shows that such predication does not in any way alter or vary the subject of the relation. By the first principle Boethius intends to explain the unity of the Trinity: in saying the Father is God, the Son is God, and the Holy Spirit is God, one is not counting three "Gods" but enumerating what is in actuality one substance. By the second principle Boethius shows that among the persons of the Trinity there is this distinction alone: though the three persons do not differ in substance, one is not the other.

The second of the theological treatises of Boethius upon which Clarembald composed a gloss is entitled *Quomodo substantiae in eo quod sint bonae sint cum non sint substantialis bona.* The argument which Boethius sets forth herein is one which he discussed with his circle of intellectual companions at one of their weekly meetings, hence its common title *De Hebdomadibus.* Boethius attempts to prove that created substantial things are good not inso-far as they exist, that is, substantially good, as is God, but they are good in-sofar as they derive from a First Good who is indeed the God who created them. The argument is presented in the style of the mathematician or geo-metrician, as it were, in that it proceeds on the basis of a set of nine axioms comprehensible only to the wise (*quoad sapientes*) which Boethius intro-duces at the beginning of the text and to which the succeeding points of his argument refer for their proof.[14]

Of the three remaining theological treatises, Clarembald makes some brief remarks only on the fifth, *Contra Eutychen et Nestorium.* This lengthy treatise presents the orthodox teaching on the true nature of Jesus Christ as God and man and refutes heresies, especially those of Eutyches and Nes-torius, concerning that doctrine. Eutyches claimed that two natures could not coexist in one person; therefore in Christ the human nature ceased to exist when the divine nature came into him. Nestorius, on the other hand, claimed that a person can have only one nature; therefore in Christ there are two persons, each with its own nature. Clarembald cites this treatise and offers some brief remarks based on it in his commentary on Genesis 1 to show that an erroneous understanding of creation can result in the afore-mentioned heresies.

The remaining *opuscula* are the *Utrum Pater et Filius,* which discusses the question of the common substantiality of the three persons of the Trinity and is a somewhat condensed review of the material in the first treatise on the Trinity, and the *De Fide Catholica,* which is a summary of Catholic dogmatic teaching. Clarembald does not mention either work in his glosses.

Clarembald's master Thierry did not leave any glosses on these last three treatises either. Gilbert of Poitiers, against whom Clarembald writes in the *De Trinitate*, did produce a gloss on the *Utrum Pater et Filius*, although Clarembald seems to be unaware of this.[15]

By the mid-twelfth century glossing the theological treatises of Boethius was an academic activity with a strong tradition spanning at least three centuries. Ninth-century figures such as Gottschalk of Orbais, Hincmar of Rheims, Ratramnus of Corbie, and Johannes Scotus Eriugena were familiar with and incorporated comments on the *Opuscula Sacra* in their writings.[16] The earliest set of complete glosses on the treatises dates from that same era and was for a long time thought by many, including Clarembald, to have been the work of Remigius of Auxerre.[17] Known as the *Auxerre Commentary*, it offers glosses on each of the *opuscula*, usually following the form of brief interlinear comments, sometimes in fact only giving synonyms for the Boethian terms. It does not offer any kind of extended discussion of the texts. Nonetheless it was accepted as the preeminent study on the treatises until the twelfth century.

The form of commentary used by Clarembald was that of his master Thierry and also of Gilbert, bishop of Poitiers. Quotations of one or more verses of the Boethian text were followed by notes and comments which explicated the passage. Sometimes these comments simply restated the meaning of the passage; sometimes they developed the thought of the passage with elaboration of detail and/or citation of authoritative sources; sometimes they offered an excurus on a related subject.

Clarembald clearly adhered to the received Neoplatonic tradition of the Chartrian school and to the general doctrinal interpretation of Thierry's Boethian glosses. This adherence is manifest early in *DTr* when Clarembald affirms in his *Introduction* 9–10 his acceptance of the position of his masters Thierry and Hugh on the question of separated forms. In discussing the etymology of the term *mathematica*, Clarembald reviews the position of some thinkers that forms do not and cannot exist apart from matter. He himself does not agree with this position, which reflects the Aristotelian nominalism of Peter Abelard and Gilbert of Poitiers, the "bêtes noires" of his gloss. Rather he quickly summarizes his view that reason was given to man that he might discern not only good from evil and true from false, but universal natures from particular ones. Thus separated forms not only exist but can be known. Even when Clarembald uses Aristotelian definitions, he remains a Neoplatonist, as when he defines a predicate (see the discussion below).

Clarembald's two glosses not only follow the style and doctrinal interpretation of those of Thierry of Chartres, but sometimes he prefers to quote Thierry, without proper acknowledgment and at length, rather than offer an interpretation in his own words, as the notes in the translation will indicate. This is the case, for instance, in his explanation of the Son as the equality of the Father who is unity in *DTr* II.34 ff.

Clarembald even follows Thierry when Thierry goes astray. This occurs in the discussion on number theory in *DTr* II. In his attempt to explain the Trinity, Boethius introduces a distinction between the numbers by which we count and the numbers which exist in numerable things. His point is that the former lead to plurality but the latter do not. Thus when saying Father, Son, and Spirit of the Trinity, one is not multiplying unities but rather only reciting a repetition of the one same thing.[18]

Thierry, while citing precisely the Boethian distinction between numbers that produce plurality and numbers that do not, proceeds in his commentary to define and discuss them in just the opposite order. In Thierry's understanding it is the numbers which exist in numerable things which lead to plurality, while the numbers by which we count do not.[19] Clarembald not only follows Thierry in discussing this distinction, but he confuses the reader further by blithely concluding his discussion with a rehearsal of the very Boethian definitions his commentary has reversed!

One can offer an account of this manipulation of terms and definitions by Thierry which his student Clarembald copied. Thierry's explication refers to the number theory proposed by Augustine, although it is Clarembald not Thierry who cites the appropriate passages in the *De Musica* (VI.2) which was attributed to Augustine in the Middle Ages. Boethius, on the other hand, was quite possibly basing his number distinctions on an Aristotelian work, *Physics* (I.2), which was not yet available to Thierry and his contemporaries. It may be that Thierry, and also Clarembald, saw themselves correcting the "mistake" of the Boethian discussion. Nonetheless it is curious that neither of these twelfth-century writers mention the fact that they are in fact reversing the terms and definitions to fit the received Augustinian doctrine.[20]

A more serious indication of Clarembald's dependence on Thierry which could lead to the conclusion that Clarembald might in fact not be at all concerned with any significant doctrinal issues is his oft-repeated insistence in his *DTr* gloss that enough has been said about a particular issue and the reader should be content with what is given and move on, even if the issue appears to be unresolved. This happens, for example, when Clarembald is discussing the notion of predicates in *DTr* IV. Before glossing the Boethian text itself, Clarembald offers a lengthy discussion in which he reviews several theories of predication. He concludes with a brief summary of his comments and states that he will adopt the Aristotelian definition. But then he adds the following disclaimer: "We do not refute the remaining senses as reasonable enough, except that which [defines predicates as] aired in sounds alone. Behold, what a predicate is seems to have been satisfactorily explained" (IV.13).

But this can hardly be satisfying to the reader since the claim of adhering to the Aristotelian definition appears to be made for the sake of convenience, not because it is true. Clarembald's Neoplatonic-inspired stipulation at the end of the passage seems to negate the full import of the definition. Further Clarembald will conclude several discussions with the same injunction: e.g., "But it would seem that enough has been said about this" (I.27) and "For the sake of brevity we are inclined not to reproduce these sources at the present time" (IV.60).

Why is Clarembald so ready to move along and leave either important questions unanswered or significant doctrinal issues sufficiently ambivalent that it is difficult to determine precisely what his position is? One possibility is that he is not entirely comfortable with the material, that he does not fully comprehend it, and therefore that he is unable to explain it satisfactorily. Rather than show his inadequacy, he congenially encourages the reader to keep moving along.

At the same time it may be that Clarembald has his commentator's sights set on something rather definite and therefore he does not want his reader delayed by complicated details to which he would be welcome to return at his leisure. This interpretation has some merit. For example, in the case of predication theory referred to above, Clarembald is very concerned lest the integrity of the Divine Being be compromised by a theory of predication which would allow for diversity of any kind within the Divine Being itself. Thus he is not interested so much in setting forth a precise theory of predication as in making the reader aware of what an unacceptable theory would be. But why is this the case? What is Clarembald's project?

Unlike Thierry, Clarembald offers at the beginning of each of his glosses substantial introductory comments which specify the context of his gloss on that *opusculum* and which enable the reader to appreciate the nuances of Clarembald's comments. Clarembald's purpose in glossing Boethius is not another attempt at a practice common in the medieval schoolroom. Clarembald has rather a clear and decided apologetic purpose, especially in the *DTr*, aimed at countering the suspect interpretation of Gilbert of Poitiers, whose glosses were condemned by the Council of Rheims in 1148. It will be remembered that the original request for a gloss from Clarembald arose because of the doctrinal and stylistic problems encountered in the good bishop's gloss by certain religious. Clarembald has set for himself the task of explicating the Boethian text in the context of that request. His style and his choice of issues to address is governed by that project.

A case can also be made that Clarembald also was concerned to confront other opponents. Among these is Peter Abelard, who is pointedly accused of reintroducing the heresy of Arianism. Clarembald's comments on Abelard are drawn from Bernard of Clairvaux and he dismisses Abelard rather contemptuously and quickly.

Another opponent whom Clarembald may be confronting in his writings is a heretical sect which later came to be called Catharism. A neo-Manichean group popular in northern France and fought against at church councils by Clarembald's bishops, Cathar doctrine included a denial of the Trinity of persons, a belief that the world was the creation of an evil genius and was therefore in no way good, and a belief that Christ was neither a divine being nor in any way the creator of the world. Clarembald's *opera* address all these issues, although he never mentions the Cathars by name. Apologists of his time, such as Alan of Lille, Radulphus Ardens, and the author of the *Summa contra Haereticos,* wrote tracts against the Cathars, but Clarembald alone utilized Boethius to achieve this end.[21]

The preceding discussion seeks to account for Clarembald's informal and perhaps even occasionally chatty style, a style which may be disturbing to the scholarly reader whose interest lies more in the tightness and rigor of an argument than in the somewhat informal, persuasive style of a pastorally motivated apologetic. But before succumbing to the temptation of dismissing Clarembald as a careless and inexact scholar, however amiable in his tone, it is important to note that there are some interesting and perhaps even significant innovations in his glosses. There are two such that are deserving of attention.

An interesting innovation in Clarembald's works is his use of texts and *auctores* not used or cited by Thierry in order to explain a passage or to expand upon his interpretation of it. These include Aristotle's *Sophistici Elenchi* (perhaps the earliest citations of this work in the twelfth century), Euclid's *Geometria,* and Galen's *Tegni* and *De Elementis ex Hippocrate.* Such references indicate Clarembald's efforts to bring to bear in his glosses on Boethius the latest resources available to him as well as the extent of his own personal reading and study.[22]

A second and perhaps the most significant innovation on Clarembald's part is his understanding of the relationship between philosophy and theology. Clarembald adheres to the traditional view expressed by Thierry and others: philosophy contains all knowledge and under its branches all areas of intellectual inquiry are subsumed. Clarembald offers two divisions of philosophy in his *Introduction* to the gloss on the *De Trinitate*. The first is the division found in Thierry's *Commentum* which follows the Stoic model.[23] Philosophy has three principle branches, following the three natural activities of man: thinking, speaking, and acting. Corresponding to the first activity is speculative or theoretical philosophy (*philosophia speculativa*); to the second, logic or disputative philosophy (*philosophia rationalis sive sermocinativa*); to the third, moral philosophy or ethics (*philosophia moralis*).

Clarembald then offers a second division of philosophy based upon the Aristotelian distinction between theoretical and practical knowledge. This principle of division is mentioned by Thierry, but is not elaborated upon as it is by Clarembald.[24] In this division, Clarembald notes, it is important to realize that there is theory (knowledge of principles) and practice (knowledge of operation) in all the divisions of philosophy. Theoretical philosophy *per se*, however, is subdivided into mathematics, physics, and theology. Practical philosophy is divided into private (governance of the individual), economics (governance of the home), and politics (governance of the state). Clarembald offers confirmation for this division in the cloak of Lady Philosophy, described by Boethius in *De consolatione philosophiae* (Ip1) as having a Θ on the top hem of her mantle and a Π on the bottom hem, signifying both theoretical and practical knowledge as the two principal aspects of philosophy.

Clarembald adheres to the Boethian view that the theoretical branches of philosophy are distinguished by the manner according to which they operate. Physics examines things which consist of a conjoining of matter and form; thus this science is called inabstract because it does not abstract matter from form in its considerations. Physics proceeds *rationabiliter*, that is, according to reasonable opinion, for as things conjoined of matter and form are constantly in motion and subject to change, so knowledge of them "does not hold the necessity of truth anymore than matter holds the stability of permanence."[25] Mathematics considers the immutability of things inasmuch as they are abstracted and isolated from matter, although they do not in actuality exist apart from matter. Thus mathematics must proceed *disciplinaliter*, that is, systematically, inasmuch as its objects (e.g., lines) are more obscure and subtle than those of physics (e.g., changes in physical bodies).

Theology considers the Pure Form of God and the disembodied forms of created things which exist in the mind of God. These objects are entirely separate from matter and are thus completely immutable. Theology can proceed in one of two ways. In the first way theology can use images and similes and analogies from the natural universe to explain God. This method is very dangerous in theology, inasmuch as errors and heresies can arise from mistaking the natural images for the reality, which is not at all material and exists completely apart from matter. Clarembald, following Boethius and Thierry, rejects this particular method.

Secondly theology can proceed *intellectibiliter*. The term itself is difficult to translate. Unfortunately rather than offering a clear definition of the term, Clarembald contrasts it with the aforementioned theological method which attempts to approach a knowledge of Pure Form and the disembodied forms of things in the Pure Form by means of natural similes and images. Indeed even to say "God exists" is to speak in a way radically different than saying "a man exists." Thus *intellectibilitas,* to use the nominative form of the word which Clarembald employs more frequently than the adverbial, is a means of knowing God as Pure Form and the immutable forms of things which exist in the mind of God, at least to the extent of being able to determine that natural images are inaccurate and misleading. *Intellectibilitas* then is the preferred method of theological discourse. It is a supra-rational power which seems to infuse knowledge of divine things into the mind. Clarembald unfortunately does not offer a more precise definition of this term, save that it enables a man to "contemplate the divine essence itself without any material subject."[26]

Clarembald may give the reader some further insight into this meaning of this term when he presents a physiological explanation of the three operations of the mind and that physical instrument of the mind proper to each operation. In this he imitates his master Thierry and other Chartrian colleagues who were interested in explaining the world according to natural processes, as both authors do, for example, in their commentaries on the six days of creation. Imagination, which is the likeness of external things sensed by the five senses, uses "a lot of air with a little humor enclosed in the phantastical cell of the head." Reason, from which the sciences of physics and mathematics arise, uses "a most refined breath, which the physicists call 'ethereal light,' with a humor proper to it enclosed in the logical cell of the head."[27]

Intellectibilitas, however, which is that power of the mind according to which the science of theology must proceed if it is to comprehend the

Pure Form itself and the disembodied forms in the Divine Mind, and if it is to avoid the errors to which natural images are prone, lacks any such physiological instrument. This is because its objects, God and the forms of created things, are entirely immaterial and thus cannot be grasped by anything which suffers the contagion of matter. It is disappointing, even unsatisfactory, that Clarembald says no more than that *intellectibilitas* lacks any physical instrument. Nonetheless it is clear that because of *intellectibilitas* theology is quite unique among the sciences. Even though it remains a part of philosophy, it is clearly distinct from the other two speculative sciences.

Clarembald emphasizes this distinction in another rather interesting way: he transfers the term *intellectibilitas* from the *De Trinitate* gloss to that on the *De Hebdomadibus*. Boethius had only used the term in his second commentary on Porphyry's *Isagoge* to explain how that which is completely apart from matter can be known.[28] Thierry had originally introduced the term into his discussion of the *De Trinitate,* although the term does not appear in that particular Boethian text, in order to explain how theology proceeds.[29] Clarembald uses the term in the same way as Thierry in his gloss on the *De Trinitate,* but then introduces it into the *De Hebdomadibus* gloss, explaining that it is only by *intellectibilitas* that one can grasp those common conceptions of the mind or *per se nota* which are presented by Boethius as the axioms upon which the solution to the question raised in that treatise can be answered, namely, whether things which are good are substantially good.

Clarembald's use of the term *intellectibilitas* may well be connected with his apologetic concerns, for the term conveys the mind's reliance on an external source for confirmation and validation of statements about the nature of God and about the relation of God to creation. This is necessary because reason, which for Clarembald (and Thierry) operates on the basis of a certain physiological instrument, is by that very fact incapable of grasping knowledge of what is completely immaterial. Perhaps this emphasis on the absolute need for the power of *intellectibilitas* is one way for Clarembald is dissociate himself from those who have clearly erred in their explanations of God by using natural images. Without this power, man must rely solely on reason and sense, and therefore on explanations based upon such reasoning. The light of *intellectibilitas* enables man to judge the appropriateness of the images, which are naturally prone to error, even grave error, because that which he tries to imagine is pure form and immaterial. What is divine and what pertains to an understanding of the divine as it exists in itself can only be known by *intellectibilitas* and therefore must be explained *intellectibiliter.*

For example, the axioms make assertions about being itself (*ipsum esse*), which Clarembald identifies with God, and its relationship to what exists (*id quod est*), which Clarembald identifies as created things; thus the axioms can only be understood *intellectibiliter*.

The use of this term in the *De Hebdomadibus* gloss further separates theology from the other speculative sciences. Its use is a clear indication that the Boethian *opusculum* is to be understood as a theological treatise. This Clarembald does perhaps to correct the view of Gilbert of Poitiers, expressed in his gloss on this *opusculum,* that the axioms, and perhaps also the entire text, can be understood as well by a natural philosopher as by a theologian.[30] Clarembald remarks, on the contrary, that the axioms and the text itself must be understood more theologically than according to any other faculty.[31] Indeed those axioms which are the preserve of the learned are known by them only by the power of *intellectibilitas.*

Thus Clarembald presents his view that theology holds an exalted and unique place among the speculative sciences on the basis of its power of *intellectibilitas* according to which the theologian knows what he knows about the Divine Being and the disembodied forms in the Divine Mind. Regrettably Clarembald does not offer an explanation on how the power of *intellectibilitas* operates, nor does he propose a clear distinction between philosophy and theology. Nonetheless his explanation of theology's operation is innovative.

There is no record of the reaction of Clarembald's original readers to his glosses. The small number of manuscripts indicate a very limited distribution. At the same time it is interesting that the only known citation of a passage from one of Clarembald's glosses is one which is concerned with the division of philosophy discussed above. This instance is found in the writings of no less a personage than Meister Eckhart. Bernhard Geyer has shown that Eckhart used portions of Clarembald's *Introductio* to the *De Trinitate* gloss in a sermon which was given in Paris in commemoration of St. Augustine.[32] Eckhart is explicating the meaning of the verse "Vas auri solidum ornatum omni lapide pretioso" (Ecclesiasticus 50.10) and explains the adjective *pretiosus* in terms of the three sciences of theory, logic, and ethics.[33] Then Eckhart says that teachers have divided the science of philosophy in this threefold way on account of the three human activities of thinking, speaking, and acting:

> Sic enim dividunt nobis magistri scientiam philosophiae, scilicet in theoricam, logicam et ethicam sive practicam. Et hoc secundum illa tria,

quae ita vicissim occupant homines, ut nunquam aliquo tempore ab aliquo istorum trium feriari videantur; et ea sunt cogitatio, locutio et operatio.[34]

Geyer correctly points out the resemblance of the last sentence to the opening comment in Clarembald's *Introductio*:

Tria sunt quae hominum vitam ita vicissim occupant ut nullo tempore ab aliquo trium feriari videatur. Ea autem sunt cogitatio, locutio, operatio.[35]

Other statements that follow these opening lines of Eckhart's sermon, which present the Boethian explanation of the particular method of each science, likewise copy from other passages of Clarembald's *Introductio*.[36]

Clarembald is never mentioned by name in this sermon, nor has any other passage of this gloss or his other two works been identified in Eckhart's writings. The relevance of the *Introductio* here is obvious, but its inclusion is puzzling. Where did Eckhart acquire the text? Why did he not identify its source? Did he have access to Clarembald's other works? Further investigation into the possibility of other uses of Clarembald by Eckhart might yield additional information on this issue. It should be noted, in any case, that what is borrowed by Eckhart is a rather traditional understanding of the division of the sciences and that he is using these passages simply as a prelude to his comments on the perspicacity and wisdom in the works of St. Augustine in seeking an understanding of God and in pursuing virtue. It would be a highly speculative venture then to try to claim any notable influence of Clarembald on Meister Eckhart, who perhaps may only have copied some passages from Clarembald's *Introductio* because they were useful in expressing his thoughts on the division of philosophy and because they were for some reason available to him.

To summarize: Clarembald unquestionably eludes categorization as a mere repeater of the doctrines and style of his acknowledged master. While he does often agree with the interpretation of Thierry, he does this not out of an inability to understand the passage but because he finds that interpretation apt. In this Clarembald holds a further interest for the student of medieval intellectual history. How a master's ideas were passed along by his students is an important element in understanding and appreciating the influence of a master in the history of thought. One finds in Clarembald an example of the transmission of the interpretation and understanding of one of the great minds of his time on the theological views of Boethius. Yet although his is the work of a devoted student and strictly orthodox Christian, as his writing bears witness, Clarembald nonetheless had his own purposes and ends in mind when composing his glosses.

It should be noted finally that an examination of Clarembald's works and his significance in intellectual history must also take into account his career as an ecclesiastical administrator. In this role he would be concerned, in part at least, with the true exposition of the Catholic faith for which Boethius was an accepted and revered authority. Clarembald expresses in his writings a great sensitivity to heresies both old (Arianism) and new (Catharism) and to doctrinal errors (such as found in Peter Abelard and Gilbert of Poitiers) which compromise the fullness of the Church's teaching on the Trinity, the goodness of creation, or the doctrine of the "two natures in one person" in Christ. Clarembald's apologetic efforts in his glosses then may derive as much from the concerns he had as a church official as they do from his intellectual curiosity.

In these and other instances which the notes to the translation will point out, Clarembald offers some original and interesting insights into the Boethian treatises, despite his otherwise strong reliance on Thierry. Clarembald does not merely rehearse the doctrines of his masters: he uses his learning to meet the Boethian text in a manner which will clarify for his readers issues even of his own day and he does this in a style that is uniquely his own. This sets him in a special place in the tradition of commentaries on the *Opuscula Sacra,* for his glosses are not just academic exercises and suggest the concern of Clarembald that Boethius's explanations of some of the central doctrines of the Christian faith be explicated in a clear and accurate manner for his time.

A Note on the Latinity of Clarembald's Glosses

Clarembald's language and style share much with other writers of the twelfth century. While he had read such classical authors as Cicero, Virgil, Seneca, and probably Plautus and Terence as well as the early church fathers, especially Augustine and of course Boethius, his language reveals very little in the way of classical influence. His sentences are for the most part simple in form and syntax. Even when he holds forth with his greatest rhetorical flourish, for example in his letter to Odo, one cannot find anything approaching a true Ciceronian period. When he does try to build *amplitudo* he does so by simple parataxis, that is, he will set relative clause next to relative clause, perhaps even vary it with a participle clause here or there, but each unity will be a syntactic and semantic whole.

His vocabulary too is early "scholastic." It differs, however, from later scholastic Latin in that many of the phrases (e.g., *esse quod esse*), which by the time of Thomas Aquinas become set vocabulary items to describe common philosophical notions, are not yet fixed. One senses that Clarembald is still groping for ways to express what for him and his generation are still fairly new ideas and novel philosophical methods. Moreover his text is peppered with Greek words and phrases which have not yet become naturalized into Latin. For Clarembald they still have the feel of the exotic.

Clarembald is very conscious of keeping his style simple, personal, and accessible with an eye toward his audience lest he, like Gilbert, be accused of an unapproachable style. Indeed Clarembald comments frequently on the troubles that an overly learned diction and style can cause for one writing on the subject of the Trinity. One can find three distinct styles in Clarembald: an epistolary, an introductory, and an exegetical. The two letters which we possess by Clarembald are higher in tone and a bit more formal than his exegetical writings. The sentences are a bit longer and the vocabulary much more elevated and diverse. His introductory and exegetical passages differ little in sentence structure or vocabulary. In both the vocabulary is simple and the sentences short, almost staccato. The main difference is that in the former the flow of thought between sentences is more coherent. Conjunctive particles (*enim, igitur, nunc, ergo, idcirco, quod,* etc.) have clearly discernible semantic functions. He uses them to develop his argument which is cohesive with little digression, whereas in his exegetical passages, Clarembald will use these particles indiscriminately as simple ejaculations, much like the American "well . . ." or "so. . . ."

Indeed the single most striking feature of Clarembald's language in his exegetical portions is its informal chatty quality. The Latin reads like a lecture. Clarembald the master is guiding us his students through the text. He comments as ideas occur to him within the context of his overall apologetic project. He digresses as his interest and fancy move him or as his judgment about our need to be informed about collateral ideas compels him. Yet the effect is more personal conversation than didactic. There is much in the way of humor, especially in clever word plays or gaming on (assumed) etymological origins of words. Clarembald very much enjoys puns.

It is clear that Clarembald intends to interject himself into his text in such a way that his readers will be able to follow the sometimes complicated arguments of the Boethian treatises, to avoid the suspect interpretations which are the result of a convoluted style such as Gilbert's, and to discard with distain the heretical positions of Abelard and others. And all this will be accomplished in a pleasant and affable style which seeks to bring even the slowest of learners into the hidden depths of the most intimate of the philosophical disciplines.

A General Outline of Clarembald's

Gloss on Boethius's

De Trinitate

[The numbers in parentheses refer to Häring's edition]

Letter to Odo

Clarembald's Introduction

The Prologue

A General Outline of Clarembald's

Gloss on Boethius's

De Hebdomadibus

[The numbers in parentheses refer to Häring's edition]

The Gloss of
Master Clarembald
on
Boethius's Book

De Trinitate

Letter to Odo

1. Once after I had been called to oversee his school by the bishop of Laon who still presides in that city, I was observed inhaling deeply in the abodes of philosophy.[1] For one day I had gone with a few friends to the monastery of Saint Vincent to look at the church archives.[2] While there the abbot asked me how the Creator breathed the breath of life into the face of the first being. After I had answered this question to the abbot's satisfaction, he exclaimed, "Oh, how I wish you would examine Sacred Scripture as eagerly as you passionately devote yourself to the study of the writings of pagans like Aristotle and Boethius."[3]

2. Smiling I explained that Aristotle was indeed a pagan, but then I went on to prove from Boethius's own works that he was a powerful confessor of the Christian faith. Delighted at this answer, the abbot began to beg me most persistently to compose for him some treatise concerning Boethius's *De Trinitate*. I would perhaps have neglected the abbot's request had it not been for the subsequent entreaties of many of my own confreres who were complaining about the difficulties they were having with the confusing expressions and convoluted style of the bishop of Poitiers's surviving gloss on the *De Trinitate*.[4]

3. Thus because the pious request of the aforementioned abbot coincided with that of other religious, I have attempted to explicate that question concerning the Trinity of Persons and the Unity of Substance which Boethius wanted to set out for Symmachus against the Arians.[5] It is not that I was overconfident in my own abilities, but

rather that I intended to rehearse the interpretations of my teachers, Thierry of Brittany and Hugh of St. Victor, with whom I had worked quite assiduously on this very text.

4. I designate you, then, my beloved friend Odo,[6] to be examiner and judge of my labors.[7] Indeed I am confident that if in any place I have gone off track, you will correct and reprove me objectively (yet mercifully!). With you I know that no oil of adulation will anoint my head which would perhaps easily happen if I were to entrust that judgment to one who is inexperienced in the arts and theology, since one unworthy of this honor would glory just in the fact that he had been chosen to judge this work.[8]

5. I, however, lack any such fear concerning you, since true friendship drives out all adulation. Indeed the experience you have gained by the study of the arts and theology guarantees that you will be a perspicacious judge. Thus if anything seems to need correction, you will correct it; if it is said truly according to the Catholic faith, you will approve it. These two things are not easy to do, for although there is one true teaching method which lacks falsehood, there are five counterfeit and fallacious methods that oppose the truth, yet feign to paint themselves with the color of truth.[9]

6. The first of these is called a "sterile" method, the second a "wrapping of trivialities," the third "untrained opinion," the fourth "bent exposition," and the fifth "ambiguous reasoning." Now the first two teach the truth but to no end. The others, however, can indeed produce outright falsehoods. The "sterile" method is that which does not present one with the whole of the proposed matter. For example, if a teacher using this method wanted to maintain that every essence *exists* in God, he would say, "God *knows* every essence." Any old hag is capable of this sort of trick.

7. A "wrapping of trivialities" is when, under the guise of a philosopher, someone gropes for poetic phrasing as a cover-up for his lack of knowledge, even though the argument can be stated simply. For example, if someone should wish to say, "Corporeality without the pre-existing form of a body does not appear in matter," he would instead say, "The queen is not in her bridal chamber without an accompanying handmaid." And so he wraps the truth in trivialities in such a way that he seems to have dreamt on Mt. Parnassus.[10]

8. "Untrained opinion" is what many scholars to this day shrewdly pass off on their audience so that they might acquire for themselves as

large an audience as possible. Even though these scholars are well versed in the truth of the arts, they silence that truth. An example of these is the Stoics of old who claimed that because God foresees everything, everything comes forth of Necessity. This easily convinces untrained minds.[11]

9. "Rash" or "bent exposition" is when one claims that he is a stone because he is classed together with stone in the highest genus, saying that one ought to look at the meaning, not the words.

10. "Ambiguity" is when one inserts into his words multiple implications so that he may seem to agree with many in his thinking. The true method and the one to be followed is careful that none of these five vices mixes with it. It is not easy for one to distinguish these different approaches, and so I place this work in your care for judgment.

Introduction

1. There are three things which occur in the life of men in such a way that at no time do the three seem to be separate from one another. These are thought, speech, and action. Reason, as occasion demands, regards each one of these sometimes as the same, but more often it treats them separately, as if they were drawn apart from one another. The mind indeed does not know how to be idle. Its primary task is to think over and reason out in itself whether things are frivolous or serious, then to commit to speech what has been thought over, dissected, and examined. Those things if they are reasonable ought all the more to be chosen and brought into action. If they are stupid, they ought all the more to be avoided and not brought into action.[1]

2. The first philosophers set out three branches of learning, aptly accommodating them to the three aforementioned functions: speculative philosophy for thought, moral philosophy for action, and logic or rhetoric for speech. The first of these skills the Greeks called "theoretical," the second "practical" or "ethical," and the third they designated "logical." But skipping over the logical and ethical, we shall divide the theoretical until we have reached that part of it under which Boethius's small book no doubt belongs.

3. So the theoretical or speculative is recognized to have three parts: mathematics, physics, and theology. But before going any further we must say something about the words "theoretical" and "practical." For while under the term "theoretical" one would find mathematics, theology, and physics, and under "practical" private life, economics,

and politics, nevertheless theory and practice are applied to both divisions so that in each of these arts the appropriate speculation and operation will be respected.

4. Now the theoretical is divided into the three aforementioned parts. The science of mathematics isolates from matter the quantities of bodies and the forms and figures actually inherent in matter. Physics explains the causes of the qualities, the quantities, and even the motions of bodies. Theology contemplates *intelligibiliter* the ideas of the universe which are found in the Divine Mind before they come forth in bodies.[2]

5. Practical science is also divided into three parts, namely the private, the economic, and the political, each of which serves it in a different way. The private teaches and provides for a reasonable governance of the individual; the economic, for the provision of household matters; the political, for the governance of cities and defense at home and abroad.

6. Further that part of theoretical science which is called "theology" some call "contemplative" insofar as its provenance is the sacred writings. And when they turn to the three parts of practical science, they call them "active." Boethius elsewhere recalls these two faculties when he describes the cloak of Philosophy, noting that the Greek letter *pi* was inscribed on the hem of her mantle and the letter *theta* on the collar, signifying the excellence of theology and the manifold vexations of the active life.[3] But in the rest of the liberal arts and even in the technical arts, the theoretical is nothing other than the contemplation of rules and reasons by which one must perform each art. And the practical is the science of acting according to those very rules and reasons which have been set forth.

7. It is therefore clear from these diverse ends and duties that "theoretical" and "practical" are applied in one instance to one set of meanings, but in another instance to another set of understandings. Now since it was said before that theology contemplates the forms which owe nothing to matter, and since the author himself will say in what follows that "it is the duty of each and every learned man to attempt to fashion his faith according to reality,"[4] and further since the Divine Form is outside matter, and finally since the present inquiry is about that Form: it is therefore fitting to regard this small book as theology.

8.   It must be understood that the term "mathematics" means several things. For by shortening the penultima, the word *mathesis* can be translated into Latin as doctrine or discipline, and is written with an aspiration. When the penultima is lengthened, it means superstitious divination and is written without the aspiration [*matesis*]; this may be translated as "vanity." Whence Juvenal writes: "Your birthday is known to astrologers."[5]

9.   However not all give the same reason as to why this faculty is called "doctrinal" or "disciplinary." For some assert that it is called "doctrinal" or "disciplinary" because, of all the things which are subject to this kind of speculation, there is no act which truly separates something from matter, but only a method [*doctrina*] used by teachers as if it were so. For if it were so, that abstracted thing would have a true and perpetual existence, since an abstraction is separated from matter and so has no contact with it in mutability. For it is from the nature of matter that all mutability descends upon things subject to the senses. Thus they call this faculty "doctrinal" in reference to teachers and "disciplinary" in reference to students.[6]

10.   Others say, as surely must be the truth, that reason has been naturally given to all men and thus they naturally discern good from evil, false from true, and universal natures from particular ones. But they say that no one is able to use the aforementioned power unless he acquire it through the aid of teachers, and on account of this "doctrinal" refers to teachers and "disciplinary" refers to students. These are the explanations which my venerable teachers Hugh of Saint Victor and Thierry the Breton gave me when I nagged them a little.[7]

11.   But in an inscrutable passage the master Gilbert, the bishop of Poitiers, gives this explanation. I shall present the passage here, although it might seem to be a bit lengthy, lest I seem to begrudge including such a well-known teacher with my own famous teachers. He said, "In Greek, it is called mathematics, in Latin, discipline. Both are right. Since the forms are unabstracted, that is, since they do not exist except in the concrete, it is necessary that what they are be understood. And indeed rational speculation does not grasp perfectly what it is to be something unless discipline should also grasp firmly whence it is what it is. For example: reason does not consider what it is to be a body and to be colored and to be wide unless discipline recognizes what corporeality is, what color is, what width

is. This cannot be done except it both abstract and discern these unabstracted and concrete things from that in which they exist and from one another. Therefore, because it separates what is inseparable so that the nature of those things can be looked into and their properties understood, it is called either *mathesis* or discipline."[8]

12. Enough about mathematics. Finally we should say a few words here about physics and theology, since in what follows these three speculative parts will require a fuller treatment. Physics is translated "natural": in Greek it is called *phisis* and in Latin *natura*. Its scope encompasses three areas: the terrestrial, the atmospherical, and the celestial. The terrestrial is, as they say, that which carefully examines the causes, relations, and powers of the bodies of earthly animals, especially man, herbs, and plants, as well as rocks and liquids and many things of similar qualities.[9]

13. They call that part atmospherical physics which investigates with some sophistication the causes for the changes of the air and the motions of the sea, as well as the winds and the storms and other things similar to these. They claim that that part is celestial which finely examines the nature of the celestial spheres, as well as the planets and the stars which are called "unmoved": their nature, qualities, motions, and forces.

14. But theology is translated as reasoning or speaking about the Divinity. Theology has two proper methods of reflection. Sometimes in reasoning about divine things it uses examples sought from the outside. Sometimes it painstakingly contemplates the Divine Essence itself without any material subject.

15. I speak now about examples or authorities sought from the outside. In this way Saint Augustine, when he wants to make an assertion about the Trinity of Persons, introduces a passage from Genesis: "Let us make man after our image and likeness." He wants the plural form of the verb when God says "Let us make" to imply the plurality of Persons. He wants the singular form of the nouns when the passage says "after our image and likeness" to indicate the unity of the Divine Substance.[10]

16. Macrobius likewise attests something similar about Plato who, when he was stirred to speak about God as the highest Principle of the universe, was constrained by such difficulty of articulation that he said it was as difficult to discover God to be the Framer of the universe as it was impossible to discover a fitting way to express this.

He finally fled to examples and analogies, and said that the sun, of all natural things, was most like God.[11] Now indeed in the same way those who philosophize theologically sometimes flee to examples, sometimes to similes; at other times, however, they philosophize purely and simply about the Divinity itself, not relying on metaphors of physical things so that the Divinity is free from the contagion of matter. It is in this latter way that Boethius theologizes in his treatise.

17. But now let us hasten on to what follows. It was clear above, as we recall, that this small book is placed under the class of speculative sciences because it is theological. Now it remains that I teach you about what the philosopher writes and what he intends, the reason for writing and to whom he writes, and no less the manner of writing along with the usefulness of the work and its title.[12]

18. So he writes, as is obvious, about this question: how the one substance of the Deity can exist in three persons. Not surprisingly this question had been discussed a great deal well before the time of Boethius; it had been fought against at the Council of Nicea by Arius and defended by Alexander the bishop of Alexandria and likewise by Alexander the patriarch of Constantinople, and after them by Athanasius and others down to our own day. Indeed it is said that four General Councils were convoked according to the propriety of there being four books which contain the gospels, of which one was at Nicea, another at Constantinople, the third at Calcedon, and the fourth, I believe, was at Ephesus.

19. Boethius's intention is, briefly stated, to solve just this question. The reasons for writing are as much public as they are private. Indeed the public difficulty was over a question which throws almost everyone into error. This is no wonder because, having borrowed analogies from the natural faculty, they placed grades and differences in the Deity. They were thinking that just as Socrates is said to be a man and Plato is said to be a man and Cicero is said to be a man, yet these are three different men; in the same way when the Father is said to be God and the Son is said to be God and the Holy Spirit is said to be God that these are three gods. They did not pay attention to the fact that although the Father is God, the Son is God, and the Holy Spirit is God, it is nevertheless not the case that the Father is a god other than the Son and the Holy Spirit, nor is the Son or the Holy Spirit a god other than the Father.

20. But although in the three men there is the same humanity, as will be made clear in what follows, nevertheless it is the variety of accidents that causes plurality. Wherefore it is necessary that one and the same Deity remain inseparable and invariable in three persons. This, then, was his public reason for writing. Now his private reason for writing was his family relationship with Symmachus who, with John the Deacon, I think, pleaded strongly that he explicate this question for them.[13]

21. He addresses a preface to them in which he indicates his method of writing when he says that he wants to deal with the aforementioned question according to proper reasoning and to the authority of Saint Augustine. He promises to do this in such a way that he could not be thought to be seeking popular favor or praise in any way whatever. Indeed whoever seeks popular acclaim from his writing strives and labors for this: that they, whose favor and praise he has chosen as his end, are pleased because they have understood him, which we think is the furthest thing from Boethius's intention, since much is hidden to common understanding by the style which he uses here.

22. The title of this work is marked with a notation of the Holy Trinity. It reads: "Here begins the book of Boethius about the Holy Trinity." The usefulness of this book is the knowledge of the solution of the aforementioned question and its perspicacious reasoning against the error of the heretics who, as Boethius himself will say in what follows, "having made variations by grades of merit, separate the Trinity into parts and force it into plurality."

23. But with these things having been set out, before looking at the work, let us now look at the *Prologue* which has been seen to be the most important. And may the Holy Trinity, in whose name and strength we set upon the present task, bless us that we may explain the *Prologue,* prayerfully calling on the Holy Spirit without whose gift we believe our study would be pointless, asking that his grace help us to put nothing heretical, nothing worthy of condemnation in our commentary on this book. Indeed, as the Apostle says, no one is able to say that Jesus is Lord except in the Holy Spirit. Even Cicero, although a pagan and foreign to the Christian faith, wrote something similar in his book *De deorum natura:* "No man has been great without the divine breath."[14]

Prologue

1.　"I offer to you this question which I have investigated for a very long time to the degree that the Divine Light has deemed the little flame of my intelligence worthy. I shall now communicate it to you in a philosophically and literarily acceptable form since I am as desirous of your approval as much as I was serious in my own research," etc.

Virgil in his *Georgics* tries to exalt humble things, in this case bees, with a certain poetic elaboration so that a treatise on agricultural matters might not seem trivial to his readers. Thus he calls the bees to whom certain offices have been entrusted "great-souled leaders." Seneca, too, in his little book *On Clemency for Nero,* while in some places deriding the physical weakness and the limited ability of the bee, in other places extols with lofty speech its physical strength.[1]

2.　Therefore it should not be remarkable that the philosopher who undertakes to elucidate the obscurity of the aforementioned question wants his readers to be especially attentive, since even famous scholars of our time err in dealing with this very question through their exalted self-confidence.[2] Among them is Peter Abelard, who wrote that the Father is to the Son as genus is to species, and as bronze is to a bronze ring. If one accepts this, then the Father would be greater than the Son, just as genus is greater than species. Thus by positing grades and levels of greater and lesser in the divinity, he would multiply God into gods by means of these divisions of accidents. But we shall speak against this error more fittingly in what follows.

3. Now let us turn our attention to the words of the *Prologue* and open their obscurity where the philosopher stirs attention, makes ready a willingness to learn, and obtains the goodwill of the reader. He stirs attentiveness when he says "for a long time" he had searched out the solution to the question. Indeed by saying this he indicates the magnitude and difficulty of the matter. But since this arousal of attentiveness might seem to intimidate the intellects of the readers with too much obscurity, he adds the companionship of a willingness to learn when he says that he fashioned the question "philosophically." Next he establishes goodwill for himself more securely when he says that he is motivated "neither by the seduction of fame nor the empty reputation of the common people." Indeed he gains goodwill from those persons whom he addresses when he writes that he judges them alone to be most worthy.

4. Beginning then with the magnitude of his task, he says that "for a long time" he had investigated the aforementioned question. But after he received the help of divine grace, he finally discovered that part of the question which must be held by those who conform to the true faith.[3] He eagerly sent this to Symmachus and John the Deacon, that they might participate with him in the knowledge of the question's solution and that they might show as much care and caution in verifying his solution's truthfulness as he did in studiously seeking it out.

5. Now that the meaning of these words has been clearly explained, it seems that we must review what a "question" is. A question, as Boethius describes it, is a proposition brought into doubt or ambiguity. In this regard, one needs to know that not every doubt is ambiguous nor indeed every ambiguity doubtful. That doubt which is unambiguous and is not yet shored up by reasons inclines the mind of the hearer no more to one side than to another. For example, if someone should set before me this question "Are the stars equal or not?" there is no reason or likeness to reason to incline me to either part of what is in doubt.[4]

6. So this and many such things indeed have doubtfulness although they lack ambiguity. Another type of doubt, that which has ambiguity, is separated by two opinions, one of which is true, the other only seems to be true. Both cannot be true since "every question arises out of an affirmation and its contrary negation" except in those questions in which a contradiction is prevented by either a univoca-

tion or an equivocation, or by a different manner or different part or different time or a multiplicity of relations or a figure of speech or the conditions of different predications.[5]

7. I will skip over the first six of these which Aristotle sets out in the definition of the Elenchi inasmuch as they are already very well known. But I will provide here two examples, one of figure of speech and the other of the conditions of diverse predications referring to two things, lest I incur blame by omitting too much or being too brief. A figure of speech prevents a contradiction from arising in this way: "the meadows laugh, the meadows do not laugh." The same condition of different predications referring to two things prevents a contradiction from arising in this way: if I should say "every species is more capacious than its genus, not every species is more capacious than its genus." In each example, both propositions can be true. In the first if "to laugh" is taken in its metaphoric sense as "pleasant," then the affirmative will be true which says that the meadows laugh. Also the negative, "they do not laugh," will be true if "to laugh" indicates its natural sense, namely full of laughter.

8. In the second example in which it is said that every species is more capacious than its genus, if the greater role assigned to the genus of a species is referred to in the definition, then the affirmation is true. If on the other hand in the negation, the condition of the greater role refers to the predicating principle, then the negation is also true which states that not every species is found only in its own genus. Nevertheless a contradiction could be avoided in the first example by some kind of equivocation, but in the second it certainly would be avoided by equivocation.

9. As we said before, there are two types of doubts about which questions are formed: one without ambiguity, the other with ambiguity. Aristotle has joined both, though separate, with one description, "A dialectical problem is an investigation striving either toward choice or avoidance, or to truth and knowledge, either as in itself or as supporting some other similar problem, about which there is no opinion either way or the many think contrary to the wise or they have differing opinions."[6]

10. When therefore he says "about which one can have an opinion in neither way," he is implying that type of doubt which has no answer in deductive reasoning, namely whether the stars are equal or not. When however he says, "the many think contrary to the wise or the

wise think contrary to the many," he wants to indicate that type of doubt about which there are contrary opinions. But in that place in which he says, "both think the same," he wants that kind of question to be understood which is formed out of certain propositions such as: Is a pearl a rock or not. Wherefore both in the treatise *De topicis* and in another place he notes that certain propositions are not really questions except in form.[7]

11. Indeed those questions that are constructed from certain propositions are in no way a question except in form. But those types which are fashioned neither from certain nor from ambiguous propositions have, besides the form of a question, something of its substance, namely simple doubt. Now passing over those which are not really questions except in form, two types remain: 1) that which expresses simple doubt with the form of the question and 2) that which expresses ambiguity with the form of the question. This latter ought surely to be called an absolute question. Indeed he follows Aristotle's words in the very next passage. "There are also problems about which there are conflicting syllogisms. Indeed it is doubtful as to whether they are such or not because there are plausible reasons for both sides."

12. See here he makes mention of the type of question about which plausible reasons support both sides. And he adds right afterward: "These are problems about which we have no systematic way of approaching for they are immense. It is difficult for us to assign a 'wherefore'. For example: Is the world eternal or not? For someone may well raise a question of this sort."

13. See again here he brings in those questions which are fashioned from neither uncertain nor ambiguous propositions. These indeed really cannot be called questions in the absolute sense, any more than those which have the form alone of a question while retaining nothing of doubt. Since these are clearly the three distinct types of questions, that question as I see it which the philosopher sets out to solve is a pure and absolute question: it is supported by reasons drawn on one side from the analogy of natural things and on the other side from what is held as necessarily true theologically.

14. This question is unformed, just as is every question before it is thoroughly examined to determine on which side of the contradiction the truth lies. But after he has proved by reasons and arguments which side of the contradiction must be held, he asserts that that answer is truly informed by reasons.[8]

15. Boethius continues: "You can understood how this matter presses on my mind whenever I commit my thoughts to writing both on account of the very difficulty of the subject matter as well as on account of the few people, that is yourselves, with whom alone I would speak about it." He offers the aforesaid question, which he entrusts to writing, to be judged by Symmachus and John the Deacon and no one else. "By this fact," he says, "it can be understood" that he set out to solve this question, being attracted by no vain hope for glory since he conversed with "the few," namely with the philosophers Symmachus and John the Deacon and "alone" with others like them, in language veiled to "vulgar" understanding even though the very difficulty of the "matter" itself required plain and common speech for understanding.

16. Wherefore he adds right away, "neither by a striving after fame nor empty popular applause, but if there be any external reward, it could not be anything other than to hope for an explanation similar to the matter." In the *De consolatione philosophiae* this same philosopher writes as follows against those who seek after goods or who speak not in the service of true virtue but for vainglory: "In some way the secret awareness of self-approval diminishes itself inasmuch as one in exhibiting his effort receives the payment of fame." Moreover it little becomes a philosopher to write about so hard a topic with such language that he seems to want to earn the applause and empty praises of the people just as comic actors sought to manufacture praise for themselves.[9]

17. He says, "But if any external reward," that is, the praise of human tongues, is hoped for by me from solving this question, it must be sought not from the common crowd but from theologians because, since the matter is theological, it must be supported by the judgment only of theologians, namely by you and those like you, who can determine if the matter has been expertly or inexpertly stated. Whence without interruption he adds, "So wherever I turn my eyes from you, there appears either the apathy of the dullard or the jealousy of the shrewd, so that it would appear insulting to the Divinity to propose such treatises to monstrous men who must not be acknowledged so much as trampled under foot."

18. After he says that this treatise should be entrusted to Symmachus and to John the Deacon, who are the sort of men who should judge it, he shows why he judges others unworthy to do this because, having considered them, he finds some either idle or sluggish, who

would be unprepared for this kind of examination, and others jealous and treacherous, who would prefer more to mock and vilify his treatise out of malevolence. Of these he calls certain ones idle and sluggish, namely dull and slow of mind; others deceitful and envious so that if he were to submit to their judgment his treatise on divine things, this would seem to be "an insult" to the divine things because the deformity of their vices makes them more like "monsters" than rational creatures.

19.   And therefore he immediately introduces the brevity of his style and the unusual manner of his writing in this way: "For this reason I write with brevity and hide with the meanings of new words things taken from the intimate discipline of philosophy so that they would speak only to me and to you if ever you should gaze upon them." Theology is rightly called the intimate discipline of philosophy because it has in addition to the prominent nobility of its subject matter something of a wondrous singularity for, although the other powers of the mind use their own instruments assigned to each by nature, the *intellectibilitas* which the theologian uses lacks any instrument.

20.   For sense is the first disposition of the mind engaging an external form. It uses its own proper instrument, as sight the eye, hearing the ear, smell the nose, tasting the tongue and palate, touching the hand.

21.   Moreover imagination is the likeness of sense which has been brought in through external things. It also uses its own instrument, specifically a lot of air with a little humor contained in the phantasical cell of the head.[10]

22.   Reason uses for its instrument a most refined breath, which the physicists call "ethereal light," with a humor proper to it enclosed in the logical cell of the head.

23.   But *intellectibilitas,* as has been said, lacks every instrument. Whence even Plato thought it to be of solely a divine kind and "so belonging to few men."

24.   However he calls "new words" those things which we shall find in what follows, such as "God is the form of being" and "God exists because he is but other things do not exist because they are." Or rather he is calling "new words" philosophical words to which every solution must conform, even though the Holy Scriptures are not accustomed to use them. Thus he veils the height of theology by the

novelty of such "words," so that the uncommon words "speak," that is, they have meaning, "only" to the writer and to those to whom he writes and to others like them. Thus the rest, who have not ascended to such perfection in theology and who therefore are unable to grasp it with their intellect, are judged unworthy to be deriding what they, completely removed from this text, do not know.

25. And this is what he says: "We indeed removed these others since those unable to grasp it with their intellect seem unworthy even to read it." And these things indeed happen in the aforesaid way. Now let us hear what he adds: "This ought to be pursued by you only so far as the insight of human reason is able to climb to the loftiness of the Divinity. For in the other arts the limit is constituted by that same path by which reason ascends. Medicine does not always bring health to the sick. But it will not be the fault of the doctor if he omits nothing of what he could have done."

26. In this place two readings are found and it can be explicated variously according to each of them. Some manuscripts read "sane tantum," others read "sed ne tantum." Some want to understand *sane* as "surely" and *ne* as "not;" others want to understand *ne* as "even." Now when *sane* is found in the manuscript, the passage can be explained in two ways. First as if it were saying "This ought to be pursued by you so far as," that is, you ought to seek from me as much as "the insight of human reason is able to climb to the loftiness of the Divinity," that is, as much as the contemplation of your reason, you who are men, is able to comprehend about the Divinity. Indeed it is not right that a man should ask for the solution of a question beyond the powers of the man.

27. The second interpretation would be: "This ought to be pursued by you as far as," that is, you ought to seek from me "as much as the insight of human reason is able to climb to the loftiness of the Divinity," that is, as much as the contemplation of my reason, who am a man, is able to comprehend about the Divinity. If *ne* is read as *etiam* [even], either sense of the exposition can be satisfactory. But if *ne* is taken as "not," only the first of the meanings expounded can be accommodated, so that it is read in this way: you ought to seek from me not more than the subtlety of your reason, you who are a man, can know about the Divinity.

28. *Neque enim.* As if he were to have said: There is a possibility in me to solve this as there is an inclination in you to ask. Therefore although

I cannot completely untie the knot of this question, which is impossible for a man, if nevertheless the things I shall say in the solving of the question are congruent with reason, this ought to satisfy those requesting a solution to this question. The same end is constituted for the professors of certain arts even if they do not attain that for which they greatly hope. Nevertheless if they omit nothing in the process, they will not leave any art satisfied by one honorable end alone, just as in the same way the philosopher in the fourth book of *De topicis* recalls about the end which is set for orators: "The end of the orator is at one time in himself and at another time in another person; in himself when he has spoken well, in another when he has persuaded." There is also a twofold end set for doctors: one "if none of those things which ought to be done" are omitted; another if they heal or preserve life. The same is agreed upon for professors of the other arts.

29. There follows: "But as much as this question is more difficult, so it ought to be easier to be indulgent." After he has requested from those seeking a solution that they should moderate the manner of such an ambitious inquiry, he asks that he be pardoned if he is unable to propose a satisfying solution to the question. After he has requested their indulgence, he immediately gives the authority for his work, saying he has gathered arguments from the writings of Saint Augustine by which he will strengthen his treatise.

This is the sense of this sentence: I ask your discretion as you examine skillfully whether "the seeds of reason from the writings of Saint Augustine" being something useful to you—the seeds being the principles on which especially in this question I rely, having accommodated them for us. And this is what he says: "Nevertheless you must examine also if the seeds of reasoning sown in us in the writings of Saint Augustine have borne fruit. And now let us begin on the proposed question."[11]

The Gloss

I

1.   "There are many who usurp the dignity of the Christian religion, but
that faith is especially vigorous and unique that is called catholic
or universal, both on account of her teaching of universal rules
through which the authority of that same religion is understood and
further on account of the fact that her liturgies have spread to almost every corner of the world."

    In Cicero's book *De deorum natura,* we find it written that men
were first called "superstitious" who offered sacrifices and oblations
to the gods with the intention, or rather devotion, that by divine
mercy their heirs would survive.[1] For this reason that devotion has
been called "superstition," although the word has later been in-
vested with a broader meaning. Whence among the ensuing gen-
erations people labeled "superstitious" whatever was contrary to
their own cultic practices simply because they were different.

2.   The wisest of the ancients hold that the word "religion" did not
derive from *religandus,* as some surmise, but rather from *relegendo,*
as Cicero wants to derive it, because it ought to be set in the mind
through reading.[2] The former maintain that the starting point of
the Christian religion is in the Catholic faith because it is the principle and foundation of the virtues without which eternal life cannot be hoped for by Christians. Christians also call "superstitious"

those things which seem to be contrary to the divinely established rites of the Holy Church. They call "heretical" those things which seem to be contrary or dissonant to the Christian faith which we have called the starting point of religion.[3]

3. Whence because the religion of this faith ought to be set in the mind through reading, the most Holy Church is accustomed to sing each day the hymn of Saint Athanasius.[4] Therefore when Boethius says: "There are many who cloak themselves with the dignity of the Christian religion," we ought to understand by the word "religion" that faith which must be revered and from which one who does not fear to deviate cannot be saved, just as Saint Athanasius wrote: "If anyone wants to be saved, he must hold the Catholic faith before all else."

4. Since, however, the philosopher begins with faith which is the cause of this question, we should take the opportunity to consider as carefully as possible the term "faith" since it can be used in many ways. For it can be taken as a certain belief that the Deity is three persons in one substance, as well as that God became incarnate, and many other things which are contained in the Apostles' Creed and the Athanasian hymn. But even the demons have this belief and "tremble," according to the saying of the Apostle.[5] And so there is no salvation for them because they do not love what they believe but rather hate all the more the divine virtue. And in this case faith is not to be taken for a virtue.[6]

5. On the other hand there is "faith" according to the definition of the Apostle: "Faith consists in hoping for things unseen, the guarantee of what is not apparent."[7] This faith is a virtue. Neither the demons nor the pagans believe according to this sense. For the hope of invisible things is not present in them by reason of faith. They fear more than hope for the coming of Christ.

Faith of this kind, moreover, is the first union of the mind with God because, when we receive this faith, we begin to be united to God. But we are fully united to God after we have arrived at charity. Whence ethicists assign a threefold existence to faith, hope, and charity, which, while they are three virtues, nevertheless are one thing because what we believe in this life, what we hope for in this life and in eternal life, even though in this life they are as they are understood by us, will ultimately be one in us, namely charity.[8] And so faith and hope are imperfect in us because of the defect of our mortality, not because of faith itself or hope itself.

6. A third meaning of faith is the doctrine of the Christian faith.[9] Those who "usurp" it incur grave danger, teaching it poorly and believing it sinfully. Therefore he says: "Many usurp the dignity of the Christian religion."

7. Whence it seemed to my teachers and to me following them that "the Christian religion" in this passage means the revered doctrine of the faith which saves.[10] For Arius, Sabellius, and those ignorantly following them, poorly taught and sinfully believing, stupidly claimed this faith unto their own damnation. Further, however much the heretics rage against this faith which saves and against the doctrine of this faith, it nevertheless retains its unique splendor and dignity. Because of the universal traditions of the teachers and the rules by which the value of this faith can be understood and its dignity, being defended, can be preserved, and because its worship and proclamation, according to the voice of the Psalmist, "goes out to all the world and extends to the ends of the earth,"[11] therefore this faith has been called *catholica* in Greek and *universalis* in Latin. The beautiful splendor of faith is understood by this name because in that which "is called universal" the eradication of heresy is implied. And it is called universal indeed by a likeness to universals, for just as a universal draws together all those things taken under it by uniting them into one nature in itself, so the universal faith calls to itself and unites in itself "universally" every nation, every sex, every age, and finally every creed. For neither is it solitary, as the law of the people of Israel or as circumcision is given only to males, but, as has been said, it unites and draws together all things in itself. For truly, as the Apostle says, "There is no distinction of Jew or Greek in it."[12]

8. There follows: "The belief of this concerning the unity of the Trinity is . . . ." Thus having commended the catholic faith, he adds the concept[13] of that faith about the three persons in one substance. I think I should define succinctly here the term "person": a person is an individual rational substance.[14] One should understand in this that, when we assert that there are three persons in the one essence of the Deity, we ought not to conclude there are three individual rational substances. Rather we affirm that there are three persons because they bear a certain similarity to three persons who are separated from one another. This we will show as it is in the Father and the Son, and so also as it should be understood about the Holy Spirit.

9. Therefore let there be a man who is also a father, such that at the same time he is no one's son. And let his son be no one's father. These are Adam and Abel. I speak, therefore, about the father Adam and about the son Abel because "this father is not a son" and "this son is not a father" for, since Adam and Abel are two individual rational substances, it cannot be that Adam is the son or Abel the father. Therefore, because a person is an individual rational substance and there are three persons in the Deity, they have this similarity to three individual rational substances: nothing of the three can be said universally about the others, just as Adam cannot be called Abel nor Abel Adam with their proper names. For they have only one relationship: of fatherhood for Adam, of sonship for Abel.

10. According to this analogy, I assert that these three distinctions of the Deity have to be called "persons." For the Father should not be called the Son or the Holy Spirit; if the Holy Spirit is taken relationally, neither should the Son be called the Father or the Holy Spirit, nor the Holy Spirit called the Father or the Son.

11. Now that we have set forth briefly why the distinctions of persons must be spoken of in God, we now add the Catholic concept about the unity of the Trinity: "They say the Father is God, the Son is God, and the Holy Spirit is God. Therefore the Father, Son, and Holy Spirit are one God." When I discussed the idea of a question earlier, among other things I recall that I said that the question about which this treatise is concerned is simply and absolutely a question because it is approachable by arguments: on the one hand those coming from an analogy to natural things, on the other hand those held by the necessity of theological truth.[15] Because of this contrary arguments can seem to arise. For if anyone were to pursue the analogy to natural things too far, he will readily see that it is possible to conclude that there are three gods, even though he knows that any one of the three persons is God with the same divinity as the other two.[16]

12. To be sure, Socrates, Plato, and Cicero are all men with the same humanity. But nevertheless since Socrates is a man and Plato is a man and Cicero is a man, I in no way doubt that they are three men. This should not be wondered at because, although they are men with the same humanity, nevertheless there exists a plurality of men on account of the variety of accidents. But in the three persons of the one Deity the truth is far different. For since from the very same

Deity there are three persons, God, and moreover since it is impossible for there to be anything accidental in the Deity, a plurality of gods cannot at all exist among them. It is clear, therefore, that Catholics hold the aforesaid conclusion more from theological reasoning than from analogy to natural things.

13. But since above we said that Socrates, Plato, and Cicero were men from the same humanity, although this does not support an explanation of this present treatise without much work, nevertheless because some well-known teachers have taught that individual men are men by individual humanities, we are compelled to show by a brief effort that there is one and the same humanity by which individual men are men. This will be made clear in this way: each most particular species exists in the whole substantial being of each of its individual members. No one can deny this truth unless he contradicts with impudent obstinacy both the authority of the teachers of logic and the rules of logic. Humanity is the same species as that which it is to be a man. Those who attribute individual humanities to individual men admit this with us. If, therefore, this species "man" is nothing except one thing, then the species "humanity" is nothing except one thing.

14. But here someone may object in this way: although man is nothing if not one species, there nevertheless are many men under that species. Therefore, since man and humanity are the same species, there are many humanities under the species humanity. To this objection we respond in this way: no one has heard from the beginning of time that individuals confer substantial being on anything. The substantial things are genus, species, differences, and definition. If, however, the species "humanity" is a most specific instance, no species can be subordinated to it by order of predication.

15. Therefore no single humanity of Socrates, Plato, and Cicero makes them to be men. None indeed. This will be clear to anyone who wants to philosophize truly as follows: reason knows how to perceive a thing in one way, mathematics in another. For reason always looks intently around the material thing. Whence by this intuition it judges man to be a species, as it is under the word "man." However, individual men, as they truly exist in actuality, are found subjected to this nature—man, as it is under the word "man."

16. But mathematical speculation comprehends things as they exist only under formal names and wholly other than as they subsist in

true actuality. This you may understand from this example: you may define a line to be longitudinal without being latitudinal, but there is no such actual thing to be found in the natural universe. For nothing actual can be found which has length but not width. Nevertheless the definition of mathematical speculation by which a line is said to have longitude without latitude is not useless.

17. This is also made clear from these considerations: since reason and mathematical speculation perceive the same thing, each in its own way,[17] it is not true that there are many humanities under the species humanity although there are many men under the species man. Whence also to the genus of animal, nothing lower is added, as it is subjected in this proposition: "Animal is a genus." For it is subjected mathematically; this is why the proposition is called a singular proposition. As the same genus is predicated in this proposition, "A man is an animal," certainly man is subjected rationally for all animals are subjected to that genus.

18. Since the same genus may be subjected here and predicated there, according as it is subjected here it has nothing under it in the natural universe and as it is predicated there it has many natural things under it in actuality, it is no wonder that when man and humanity are the same species there are many men under the species man but no humanity is contained under the species humanity. For since man and humanity are the same species, they are unable to have opposing individuals. This would be the case if this man were an individual of this species and that humanity an individual of that species. For neither is this man that humanity nor that humanity this man. But this man is an individual instance of humanity although this species is predicated of this man not by the name of "humanity" but of "man."

19. We could set in opposition many opposing arguments. But since the intention of our work hastens us on to something else, let us return to an explanation of Boethius's next words. After these propositions he sets forth the truth of the Catholic faith: "The Father is God, the Son is God, likewise the Holy Spirit is God." Immediately after he gives the logical argument for this truth, saying: "The cause of this union is lack of differentiation."

20. Lack of differentiation is usually understood in two ways: in one way as possibility, in another as the unity of substance. We can show the first way, how lack of differentiation can be called possibility, by

drawing on examples. Let two statues be placed before us, one of bronze and the other of wood. Let us abstract in our mind the form of the bronze statue, which confers existence to that statue. Only the bronze remains. Let us also abstract that quality of bronze which supplies existence to the bronze. Only earth remains. Let us also abstract in our mind those qualities by which earth exists. But there will not be nothing which remains, even though we are unable to name it.

21. That that will not be nothing is obvious from this argument: if someone wanted to rebuild that statue by returning to it the qualities previously abstracted, it is necessary that that which is the last of the abstracted qualities be assumed as the basis to which one returned in reverse order the abstracted qualities. For there is a common axiom among philosophers that whatever is last in dissolution is first in composition.[18] Wherefore to that base, since it remained in the end when those other qualities were abstracted, after coldness and dryness and other substantial qualities of earth have been returned, there will be earth. To which, if those qualities by which bronze has its essence are returned, there will be bronze which becomes the basic matter. And having returned statuary forms to that, there will be nothing other than the initial statue. Likewise abstracting the form of the statue from the wood statue, there will remain simply wood. Having separated qualities of woodness from the wood, there will be earth. And when you have separated earth from its qualities, there will not be nothing which remains.

22. This matter is unformed: while Plato asserted it to be "between some substance and no substance," Aristotle did not hesitate to call it "an aptitude" or "a lack." Generally philosophers call it "possibility," because it can be formed in any way with the addition of a diversity of qualities. And this possibility is a certain lack of differentiation. It is not a unity in something's substance because it cannot unite anything either in substance or in accidents.

23. Although in this way the lack of differentiation cannot be taken as uniting things either in substance or in accidents, nonetheless it can be understood as the unity of the substance of the three divine persons. For the three persons are unable to receive accidents and therefore cannot be variated by accidents, it is necessary that these three be one God. And this is what he says: "The cause of this union is lack of differentiation," that is, "this union" is extrinsic, such that

it seems to arise from an analogy with natural things, because in the substance of the Deity the three persons are not differentiated and moreover they cannot be variated by accidents.[19]

24. The bishop of Poitiers wanted the force of this truth—the lack of differentiation—to arise from this alone, that in the substance of the Deity, the Father, the Son, and the Holy Spirit are the same. He assigned no force to the second part that the three persons do not differ among themselves by any variety of accidents. Yet he also conceded that the three persons were distinguished by number.

This did not seem to be appropriate to my teachers. We hold that there are distinctions, not differences, among the persons even though one is the person of the Father, another that of the Son, and another that of the Holy Spirit, that is, there is not the one same person of the three. For it does not appear sufficient to us that for that reason three persons may be one God because they are one in the substance of the Deity, for in the same way it could be concluded that Socrates, Plato, and Cicero are one man since they are one in the substance of humanity.

25. But that teacher, the bishop of Poitiers, sets up many humanities as I am given to understand from these words of his: "When it is said 'Plato is a man,' 'Cicero is a man,' and 'Aristotle is a man,' something is said not only about one man but also about his singularity, therefore something else has been said in the second affirmation than the first, and another in the third than in the first and the second. For although the second and the third repeat the name of the first predication—man—they do not repeat the thing predicated. But although like one another, the predications nevertheless affirm different natures diverse from one another in number; nay rather because they are like one another, therefore they affirm natures different from one another in number. But this necessary differentiation of the three predications concerning these three men does not allow such a unification that it might be said 'Plato and Cicero and Aristotle are singularly one man.'

26. "When therefore it is said: the Father is God, the Son is God, the Spirit of both is God, although different according to number, nevertheless they are not said to be diverse. And the repetition of the predication of a thing has been made just as the repetition of the name. And this necessary lack of differentiation of the one predicate of the three permits, nay rather compels the same three to be united in the

singularity of the thrice-predicated essence, so: the Father, the Son, and the Spirit of both are one God singularly." Thus the bishop of Poitiers.[20]

27. But perhaps he was constituting many humanities from flesh and rational spirit, defining man by that union which is the case in individual men. And so as a physicist not as a logician he asserted that there were many humanities. For a logician defines man from genus and differences, but a physicist from similar parts and activities and a rational spirit. If, therefore, he wanted to say "many humanities" because the specific parts and organs and spirit of Plato are other than those of Socrates and Cicero, all can judge how much or how well this pertains to the subtlety of logic. But it appears that enough has been said about this.

28. However because he says the three persons in God are diverse in number when he writes: "although diverse in number, they are not said to be diverse things, etc.," I dare not censure him by myself, nor do I wish to follow him.[21] For I have not been taught by my teachers nor by the writings of the ancients to differentiate anything simply by number which cannot be separated by accidents.

29. But let us hear what the philosopher adds next: "For differentiation follows those who either add or subtract. For example, the Arians variate the Trinity by grades of merits, thus they break it up and change it into a plurality. The principle of plurality, indeed, is otherness. Without otherness plurality cannot be understood."

After Boethius demonstrates by reasonable argument the Catholic conclusion that the Father and the Son and the Holy Spirit are one God since there is lack of differentiation, as explained by us above, he names those who have to confess of necessity a differentiation in the Deity. He says this differentiation is incumbent on those who "call the Father the only God in the truth of his being, the Son a creature, and the Spirit a creature of a creature."

30. And so of necessity differences of natures break up the Father and the Son and the Holy Spirit, variating them by greater and lesser degrees. So from this position it is necessary to confess that there are many gods. However these Arians have abused the words of the Evangelist which the Lord said to his disciples: "If you loved me, you would rejoice always because I go to the Father, for the Father is greater than I."[22] Note, they say, that the Son calls the Father greater than himself; and rightly so. For he is greater who brings forth, less

who is brought forth. However, they understand these things according to the flesh. Certainly the generation of the Son from the
Father is in no way comparable to human generation since it is inef-
fable. Human generation occurs by a diminishing of the substance
of both parents and a commingling of two seeds.

31. It is the madness of a demented mind to think something like this
about God. And because the Arians split apart the Trinity from
its equality by "grades of merits," namely by greater or lesser differences, with one being God and the others subordinate, so it is necessary according to them to accept a plurality of gods for "otherness
is the principle of plurality."

32. Let us tarry here a little while, pondering on this saying of the philosopher. Every composite thing has number. Moreover, every composite thing descends from simplicity. That from which anything
descends contains the principle of descent. If, therefore, duality, by
which a second thing is denominated, is created and descends from
unity, duality is not the principle of the first plurality. Nay rather the
principle of the first plurality is unity. Unity does indeed precede;
duality, by which another is counted, follows.

33. But if someone says that otherness is the principle of plurality because it precedes duality and trinity or any other greater number
subsequent to it, this would appear to be ridiculous to Boethius and
to his hearers since it is of no more use to the matter to say that
otherness is the principle of trinity than that the preceding number
is always the principle of subsequent numbers, trinity of quadrinity
and so on, one after another.

34. We will, therefore, call otherness the "principle of plurality" because otherness descends from unity as from its own unmoving
principle, so called because the first form of plurality and a certain
understanding of multitude is found in it. For just as things subject
to fate, before they are made in time, are enfolded in divine providence and exist in a certain simplicity, it cannot be known in that
enfolding what they are or how many they are or how they are. But
when they are unfolded into actuality by Providence according to
the chain of time, then their substance and quantity and quality,
as well as the place and time in which they came forth, can be
known to a certain degree. So every multitude rests enfolded in the
simplicity of unity and when in the chain of numbering a second
is numbered after one, and a third after the second and so on in the

series, then at length a certain form of plurality is understood to be flowing out from unity, and so there can be no plurality without otherness.[23]

35. For every plurality is either a duality itself, from which the denomination of otherness is taken, or it exists out of duality or another quantity, that is either unity or some multitude. Whence this same philosopher elsewhere says that every number exists either from equality or inequality because it cannot be denied that every number exists from one, which is the number of inequality, or from two, which is the number of equality.[24]

36. Since Arius comes to mind from the mention made of the Arians, as he was the leader of this sect, it seems worth noting how an ugly penalty and a divinely fitting retribution for his heresy afflicted him.[25] For the histories say that he intended energetically to persuade Emperor Constantine of his heresy. But by the intervention of divine retribution he fell to an assassin in an out of the way place and there he remained with his entrails poured out and his stomach emptied. Whence Sedulius versifies a proper derision of him:

> As empty of sense as in the time of just punishment
> He remained with entrails flowing and stomach empty.[26]

37. In our days Peter Abelard almost revived this same old heresy which had been long dormant when in a spirit full of vainglory and impiety he attempted to bring ignominy on the divinity in order to obtain glory for himself. For he wrote that the Father is the fullness of power, the Son is a certain power, namely wisdom which is the power of discernment, and the Holy Spirit is no power. Moreover there is the same condition between the Father and the Son as there is between genus and species, bronze and bronze figurines, animal and man.[27]

38. I have also read many childish things worthy of derision or rather of damnation in his *Theologia,* as he entitled it.[28] He should have entitled the book *Stulilogia*[29] if he had wanted to call it by a name appropriate to it, as the abbot of Clairvaux has written. We, however, do not have to respond to all these things, but only to certain of them because Abbot Bernard of happy memory opposed many of them expertly and derided certain of them wittily in that letter which he directed to Pope Innocent against Abelard's errors.

39. As we find in his writings, in which either he was boasting or just foolish, he hoped that power, wisdom, and benignity would distinguish the Trinity just as the persons are separated from one another by the names of fatherhood, sonship, and mutual relationship. For he wrote expressly and specifically that power pertains to the Father, wisdom to the Son. He did not admit that the Son was simply power but a certain kind of power, namely of discernment alone, and he asserted that the Father was power absolutely, which is a power equal in both generation and discernment. Whence he wants there to be that relationship between the Father and the Son which exists between a genus and its species.

40. Thus he wrote: "Since there is a bronze figurine there must be bronze, and since there is a man there must be an animal, but not the converse, so the divine wisdom which is the power of discernment exists because there is divine power, but not the converse." Let us consider, therefore, what is contained in this analogy. For either, as we guess, he wants to say that because there is the Son there *must be* the Father but not the converse, which indeed is heretical, or because there is the Son there *is* the Father but not the converse, which like the aforesaid is more manifestly a heresy.

41. Certainly there is the Father because there is the Son just as conversely there is the Son because there is the Father. Or else he wanted to conclude through a simple "there is" that if there is the Son, there is the Father but not the converse, since the power of the relation postulates the converse necessarily and equally when the consequent of the prior statement is true: if there is a Father, there is a Son.[30] Beyond this I do not know what the words of the analogy can mean. Now if another reasonable meaning cannot be found for them, the analogy (or as I more correctly call it, a disanalogy) introduced by him about the relationship of species to genus not only seems to produce nothing but also shows that the power of the liberal arts can be such in a man that he would more easily remove something theological than give up something logical.[31]

42. For since the essence of a genus always has fewer differences than a species, the substance of a species having more, how can he attribute to the Father, whom he sets up in the place of a genus, more differences, that is, of generation and discernment, while to the Son, whom he wants to choose in place of species, he attributes only the power of discernment?[32] But enough for now against Abelard. Re-

turning to the proposition let us explain how, according to Boethius, there cannot be one and two and three in the Trinity, but only one.

43. For he says: "The diversity of three or more things consists in genus or species or number. For as often as same is said, so often is diversity predicated. Same can be said in three ways: either in genus, as 'man is the same as horse because they have the same genus "animal"'; or in species as 'Cato is the same as Cicero because they have the same species "man"'; or in number as 'Tullius and Cicero are the same because they are one in number.' Wherefore diversity is said also to be either in genus or in species or in number."

44. After he taught that the principle of plurality was in otherness, he immediately shows whence otherness arose in natural things. This he does so that when the cause of otherness cannot be found in the Deity, no one can presume to assert that there is more than one deity. He says indeed that the diversity of all things and the plurality from the diversity happens because three or any number of things differ either in genus or species or number. And continuing the argument he confirms this view from a comparison of opposites, namely of diversity and identity.

45. Certainly things are said to be the same in as many ways as they are said to be diverse. But certain things are called identical in three ways, that is, either by genus or by species or by number. Wherefore things are said to differ among themselves which differ in these three ways. Those things are said to be the same in genus which, even if they differ by species, nevertheless are embraced by the same general nature, as a man and a lion in the genus animal. Other things are called the same in species which, joined in the same substantial forms, are diversified only by a variety of accidents, as Cato and Cicero under the species man. Something is called the same in number which, in order to show the signification of one singular quality, claims for itself many names, as Tullius and Cicero.

46. But it must be noted that there is not a diversity of subjects in Tullius and Cicero because Tullius is not one number and Cicero another. Therefore when we say Tullius and Cicero are the same in number, we take the verb "are" to be plural in number because of the diversity of names, and thus "the same in number" refers to a unity of substance.

For reason counts different things together with things of the same kind, so that clearly persons are counted with persons, qualities with qualities, and so forth with other things. For the subject and a form of the subject ought not to be counted together so that for instance we would count Socrates as one thing and the whiteness of Socrates as a second thing. And so if in cardinal numbering you spoke of Socrates as "one man," it would not occur to you to speak of the whiteness of Socrates as something "two."

47. At times, however, having wrongly interposed this word "thing," we call the subject one "thing" and we count a form of the subject as another "thing." But this does not come from the nature of things. For the subject and a form of the subject are actually one.[33] Nature does not produce these "things" through some natural alteration, but rather this flows from the force of mathematical consideration.[34] Nor do we correctly say "one" and "two" about the subject and a form of the subject since the subject cannot be found in reality without a form nor can a form of the subject exist without the subject.

48. Nevertheless there can be a thing of one kind among the number of things of another kind, as a man in the number of asses.[35] But he could not really be counted in their number. Since therefore things are called the same in three ways, it must be noted that those things which are called the same in genus or in species are not absolutely and simply called the same, but only those which are called the same in number. Whence Aristotle, when he first made this same division in *De topicis* about those things which are the same in genus or species or number, which were simply called "the same," put the matter this way:

49. "Without any doubt what is one in number appears to be called the same by everyone. However this appears to be taken in many ways. Properly and first of all when the assignation is the same by name or definition, as a coat to a tunic or a walking biped animal to a man. Secondly when the property is the same, as one capable of learning to a man, and what is carried upwards by nature to fire. Thirdly when it is the same by accident, as sitting and musical to Socrates. For all these things," Aristotle says, "want to signify what is one in number."[36]

50. We introduced the Aristotelian division for this reason, so that we could show what are the same in genus and species are not for that reason the same simply. But what are the same in number are the same simply. In whatever way one thing is defined as the same in number, it must not be doubted that this happens always accord-

ing to the same accidents. So that in the first place in those things which are designated one in number by name, we should teach this: this coat and this tunic with the same accidents are one in number. Therefore this coat and this tunic would become diverse in number by a variation of accidents. Likewise whatever are designated one in number by definition are the same according to the same accidents, as this man and that walking biped animal. Therefore this man and that walking biped animal would become different in number by diverse accidents.

51. Accordingly in the second place those things which are designated one in number according to properties have the same accidents, as this man and this thing which is capable of learning. Therefore a variety of accidents would make this man and this thing which is capable of learning differ in number. Now in the third place whatever are designated one in number according to accidents are the same in the identity of accidents, as Socrates and this musician. Wherefore Socrates and that musician become plural in number by a diversity of accidents.

52. Therefore it is amazing how the bishop of Poitiers could write that the three persons in God are different in number. Whence as we have commented earlier, although we fear to reprove the man, we do not wish to follow him. And now our author states clearly that difference in number happens by a variety of accidents when he says: "But variety of accidents produces a difference in number. For three men are distinct not by genus or species but by their accidents. For if I were to separate in mind all the other accidents from them, nevertheless the place of each one is different from the others which we cannot in any way conceive to be one. For two bodies cannot occupy one place, which is an accident. And so they are plural in number because they are made plural by accidents."

53. It remains from the premises that the three persons do not differ in genus or in species. But nevertheless because it can be doubted by the unlearned whether they do indeed differ in number, the philosopher therefore teaches that in the Divinity there can be no differences according to number because the Divinity is not susceptible to accidents, and only "a variety of accidents produces a difference in number." And this is proved to be correct because three men, differing neither in genus nor in species, since they differ only in number, are distinct for no other reason except accidents alone.

54. He suitably adapts the argument of this proposition in this way in order to assert the truth because if we remove all remaining accidents from them through intellectual abstraction, nevertheless it will be necessary in every way to distinguish them by place because it is impossible for the same place to be common to them. Whence he adds: "For two bodies cannot occupy one place, which is an accident. And so they are plural in number because they are made plural by accidents." That is: two bodies cannot occupy the same place singularly so that, in whichever place one of them is contained according to its circumscriptions, another of them could not be entirely contained in the same way.

II

1.　There follows: "Come, let us begin and consider each individual thing as it can be understood and grasped. For as it has been very well said, it is the duty of the wise man to try to grasp his faith according to reality." Since he had said earlier the Father is God, the Son is God, the Holy Spirit is God, he puts forth on the basis of his theological faculty that therefore the Father, the Son, and the Holy Spirit are one God. When he adds that the reason for this union is lack of differentiation, he states that he appropriately introduces this more from theology than from speculation on natural things.

2.　He says that the Arians, using an analogy of natural things, divided the divinity through plurality. Their error makes it clear that while sometimes one needs to use natural speculation, at other times one needs theological speculation. And so in order to expound the divisions of the speculative sciences with which the philosopher arms himself and how many they are according to the properties of those things subject to them, he sets forth beginning as follows: "Come, let us begin and consider each individual thing as it can be grasped" by the intellect;[1] that is, let us inspect natural and theological things by diverse means of speculation.

3.　Natural things properly and separately have a different manner of speculation from theological, just as theological things have from natural things, each according to its own sphere. This he confirms by the authority of Cicero and he explains both faculties, namely natural and theological, with a third speculative science, that is, mathematical enumeration. He assigns properties to the sciences so that in the end one will not be ignorant of how the matter must be handled in theology. The citation of Cicero here introduced is taken from Plato in that place where he says: "Language ought to be appropriate to those things about which we speak."[2]

4.　How this diversity of speculations happens and whence it comes must not be passed over in silence, especially since the speculations themselves exist in the soul and the soul "always conforms itself to its instruments."[3] For example: when it knows something through a touch of the palm or by another instrument of touching, it understands that thing to be heavy according to the ability of its instrument to measure weight. And in the same way it cannot have an understanding of things unless the matter in the subject be somehow present in the senses, so that, when the eye comprehends something standing before it, it is necessary that the image visible to the eye be spread entirely through the eye.

5. Likewise one can philosophize about the other senses so that, when the soul itself comprehends anything by hearing, it is necessary that the sound-carrying air strike the inner cavity of the ears. And when something delectable or fetid is comprehended by the instrument of smelling, that is, by the nose having inhaled air, certain bits of flesh are carried in by means of internal hairs connected with the nerves. Moreover when it comprehends something delectable or abhorrent to the taste, the nerves, which are stretched through the palate and the tongue in order to make this sense function, are stimulated by the quality of the matter introduced. And because the aforesaid instruments of the senses are heavy, the mind has obtuse knowledge through them.[4]

6. But when the soul recalls to itself anything whatsoever through the imagination, it uses a more subtle instrument in recalling its object insofar as it considers that object more subtly.[5] In the anterior part of the head, which is called the "phantastic," much air is enclosed with a little moisture on which are imprinted the figures of those things which are known through sense. The soul uses that air with a little humidity for its instrument of imagination. As much therefore as the substance of the air is more subtle than the composition of a hand or eye or nerve, so much is imaginative knowledge more subtle than sense knowledge.

7. When the soul understands anything according to the power of reason, as much as it becomes in that consideration even more subtle and perspicacious, so much will the essence of its instrument surpass in subtlety the instruments of imagination and sense. For indeed there is enclosed in the center part of the head, which is called "logistic," a most subtle air, which is called "ethereal light" by the physicists. And it has a humor suitably proportioned to itself. Whence there arises in the soul a certain power of discernment between good and evil and between universals and particulars. As much therefore as the "ethereal light" is more subtle than the air, so much the soul can discern a more subtle thing by a miniscule bit of ethereal light than through a phantasm of it.[6]

8.   When, however, the soul raises itself to some sort of understanding of the Divine Form, it can use no instrument at all because nature cannot give any kind of understanding of him who is the Creator and Maker of nature. The soul, therefore, can rise to an understanding of the Divine Form by the help of *intellectibilitas* alone. *Intellectibilitas* is solely of divine origin and according to Plato "possessed by few men," that is, as I believe, by the prophets and those who understand the invisible things of God in the Spirit of God.[7] Therefore while our natural instruments oversee our speculation on natural things, the *intellectibilitas* of divine things, which is solely of divine origin, is ordered to our contemplation of divine things and must be used in theology in the way which the author himself lays down:

9.   "For as there are three parts of speculative science, physics considers what is not abstracted or separable in things in motion. For it considers the forms of bodies with matter which cannot be separated from bodies in reality. These bodies are in motion, as when the earth tends downwards or fire upwards. And a form joined to matter has motion."

      After he has taught that the faculties must be examined in their individual parts so that he can teach how they ought to be considered in order to explain their causes and properties, he omits ethics and logic and sets down immediately the parts of speculative science, namely physics, mathematics, and theology. He shows how we must use each kind of speculation, first showing their properties to flow partly from matter and form, partly from form without matter.

10.   In the first place he says[8] that a natural thing is in motion because all mutability comes from matter, just as on the contrary every essence comes from form, because forms of their own nature are immobile. But from contact with a mutable thing forms become mobile in the same way that wood, although *per se* immobile, is moved by the mediating motion of water. Whence Moses signified matter by the name "water" when he said: "There was darkness above the face of the abyss and the Spirit of God hovered over the waters."[9]

11.   We call "natural things" here those things which exist from the conjoining of matter and form. These the physicist considers without any abstraction of one from the other, that is, of form from matter, so that what he labels as "form" within the sphere of his discipline is that which is conjoined from matter and form. Whence he concedes that any form can transfer into the opposite of itself, as it is

clear that black can come from white or illness from health. Regarding this faculty, therefore, is a verse from the poet Ovid: "He who was white in color is now the opposite of white."[10]

12. Natural philosophy is well said to be in motion because what we call nature is neither matter without form or form without matter, but is rather conjoined from matter, whose nature is mutability, and from the form inhering in it. Whence also this philosophy is aptly called inabstract because the physicist within the sphere of his discipline does not abstract from matter the forms impressed on matter. And this is what the author himself adds: "For he considers the forms of bodies with matter," etc. "And form conjoined to matter has motion," not, however, from its own nature but, as he said, from the nature of matter. The proof of the mutability of matter is evident for he says that bodies are in motion just as the earth moves downwards and fire rises upwards.

13. There follows: "Mathematics is inabstract without motion. For it investigates the forms of bodies without matter and for this reason without motion. These forms, since they exist in matter, cannot be separated from it."

The philosopher says that mathematics is without motion because it understands the forms as being abstracted from matter in their immutability. For just as physics is said to be in motion because it always considers the forms of bodies surrounded by the mutability of matter, so mathematics is rightly asserted to be without motion because it considers the forms, which do not exist except in matter, to be truly isolated from their subject. For whatever exists in matter, if it were separate from matter, as the mathematical understanding abstracts it from the subject, would be a true and perpetual essence.[11]

14. In accord with this method the philosopher in the second prologue of *Arithmetica* defines this same science to be wisdom, saying that it is the comprehension of the truth of things which exist and which receive their essence from immutability.[12] Whence because it is most difficult to understand the material in this kind of truth, it is most easy for those engaging in this discipline to become haughty and arrogant. And for this reason Pythagoras feared to call them *sophoi* [wise] when they were first called *sophoi*. But he brought them down a bit with a humbler title, having called them *philosophoi,* that is, lovers of wisdom.

15. It is a wonder that he called mathematics "inabstract" since he regards it to be without motion because it considers abstracted forms.
But as he teaches that the forms of nature abstractable by the soul
inhere in reality in matter, it is not true to say "inabstract" in such a
way that mathematics would not differ from theology. For mathematics, which in this discussion he places in the middle of the three
parts of speculative science, takes specific differences from both,
that is, from physics in being inabstract and from theology in being
without motion. A satisfactory explanation of the meaning has been
presented for the aforesaid text, so we hope. Now we turn to theology about which he says:

16. "Theology is without motion, abstract, and separable. For the substance of God lacks both matter and motion." The philosopher shows
that theology is without motion and is abstract. For this truth he immediately offers this argument, that "the substance of God lacks
both matter and motion." Therefore because the divine substance
does not exist in matter from which all mutability descends, rightly
does he propose that theology is without motion. Theology is properly asserted to be abstract as much from the mode of existence as
from the method for studying it. For the Divine Form must be investigated as it is, removed from any contagion of matter.[13]

17. There follows: "It will be necessary to consider natural things according to proper reasoning, mathematical things according to correct computation, and theological things according to *intellectibilitas* so as not to be led to images but rather to view the very form
which is true form and is not an image and is being itself and that
from which being comes."[14]

After he has listed the parts of the speculative sciences and explained their properties, he clearly adds how each one of the individual parts which are contained in the speculative sciences ought
themselves to be handled. For in physics we ought to use reason, that
is, opinion. Because if we call those things natural which are made
from matter and form, matter, then, is always in motion and flux and
therefore does not have true being. We are rightly taught to use
opinion in considering natural things because an opinion does not
hold the necessity of truth anymore than matter holds the stability
of permanence. Or it is necessary "to consider natural things according to proper reasoning," that is, by seeking the rational causes for
why this is only such, or that is hard or soft, and other similar things.

18.   The philosopher must use "mathematical things according to correct computation," namely, abstract or intellectible terms. For a mathematical consideration is more obscure by the degree to which it is an intellectual process and more subtle by the degree to which it requires the insight of reason.[15] And therefore it judges more truly in itself the quantities and figures of bodies, just as that power of the soul which considers matter judges the quantities and forms of bodies. Indeed if you were to draw a circle in water or in dust, you would depart from the truth of a circle more easily because the wavering and pliancy of the water cannot retain a circle's impression in it and a false circularity can exist in the least bit of dust.

19.   "It will be necessary to consider . . . theological things according to *intellectibilitas*," namely the *intellectibilitas* of theology, "and not be led to images." As Cicero relates in his book *De deorum natura*, Epicurus was being led to images when he attributed human form to the divinity and said that God is "quasi-corporeal" not corporeal and has "quasi-blood" not real blood. He denied that God was the maker of the created universe as if the labor of this mundane work could detract something from his most high beatitude. Whence everything is invented out of the in-between worlds, namely out of the void and atoms, with no one taking care of it and no one maintaining it. For he thought the anguish of the Divine Mind would increase if he allowed God to care for the world.[16]

20.   Some want this movement "to images" here to be directed against anthropomorphism, which holds that the divinity of the Father is contained in human form and that Christ prays for us on bended knee to the Father in heaven. But, as has been said, it is not necessary to be led "to images" in such a way that we want God to be imagined in any natural form, but rather purely, simply, and immediately to contemplate that "form which is true form." For God is not "a form" brought forth from something else as other forms are from him, because he is the form of being which other forms do not have and thus is "truly form."

21.   However the forms of the forms of those bodies, which are enfolded in God, are only images. And every form of bodies flows from that form which is the highest equality and justice. It imitates the highest form as much as it can because form is the perfection and equality of a thing above which the thing itself is not itself and below which the thing itself is not itself.[17]

If, therefore, this equality is absent from the thing itself, the thing will without doubt be a monstrosity: just as if rationality or mortality were lacking in a man, the man would be subsisting beneath his own equality, that is, being less than his definition postulates, so that he would be a monster. But if a form alien to the definition of man and proceeding beyond the mean is added to the aforesaid two forms, the addition would likewise be a monster. And therefore he says: "which is truly form and not an image and which is being itself and the source of being."[18]

22.   Here it must be noted that the being of God is not spoken of in the same way as the being of a creature. Indeed when being is said of God, it is taken substantively and it signifies the essence in which all things that exist participate. God himself in no way participates. The verb "to be" is as a proper name of the Divinity, as the Divinity itself says about itself: "I am who I am." Furthermore in Exodus one reads that when the Lord sends Moses to Pharaoh, he says "You will say to Pharaoh, 'he who is' sent me to you."[19] When, therefore, we say "God is," that verb signifies the form of being which is itself a simple entity participating in nothing. But when someone says "man is," that verb is predicated of man participatively because a man, just as every creature, is something by participation in that highest entity.

23.   Just as white is the form of being white and black is the form of being black, so that primal entity is the form of being in all other things. Moreover just as whiteness and the form of white are everywhere, and blackness and the form of black are everywhere, so something is everywhere, that is, the form of being. But something is everywhere. Therefore the form of being is everywhere. But God is the form of being. Therefore God through his being is everywhere.

Thus it is clear how that artificer-form is "truly form and being itself," that is, the primal entity, "and is the source of being" truly according to that reason by which all things that exist participate in that simple entity. Having set all this forth as best as we can, let us turn our minds to explicate what follows.

24.   For the author himself says: "Every being is from form. For a statue is said to be the image of an animal not according to the bronze, which is matter, but according to the form by which the likeness exists in it. And bronze itself is so called not according to earth which is its matter but according to the figure of bronze. Likewise

earth is so called not according to unformed matter, that is, *kata ylen,* but according to dryness and heaviness which are its forms.[20] Therefore nothing is said to exist according to matter but according to its proper form."

25.   In order to elucidate this obscure passage, my teacher introduced many philosophies.[21] From these, those which seemed to be in accord with Holy Scriptures he accommodated to this passage. For it is a wonder that the philosopher declares that "every being is from form" since individual composite things seem to be made up equally from matter and form. Whence we must examine more intently and skillfully what matter and form are.

26.   Since philosophers have called matter "possibility," possibility then is "an aptitude for receiving diverse states." For that is possible which neither follows from necessity nor from act but from both, as a certain changeability from this into that or that into this. As when I say, "It is possible for an egg to become an animal." This is the same as saying "an animal can come from an egg, but it does not yet exist and it can be impeded so that it does not happen." Such change-ability from this into that or that into this has been called by the philosophers "matter," which can be found through the abstraction of form, as we have already clearly explained in that place where we proposed to use lack of differentiation in one way for possibility and in another for the unity of substance. Therefore the use of that passage will be required here.[22]

27.   Certainly it will be found there how, having abstracted all forms from the bronze or wood statue, that which remains at the end is nothing other than a certain aptitude for receiving diverse states. And this is unformed matter which here is called "possibility."[23]

28.   Philosophers call form the "actuality" of a thing. For if something exists in actuality, it also exists in form because if it does not exist in form, neither could it exist in actuality. And likewise a thing is first called an existing thing when, because it has received a form, it can now be brought into substance. As long as it vacillates in the afore-said changeability, what the thing is or of what kind it is cannot be called by a name nor expressed in a description. On account of this, therefore, philosophers call form the "actuality" of a thing. And for that reason they agree that "every being exists not from matter but from form."

29.   But this actuality, which we have called the "form" of a thing, can be understood to exist in two ways, as either with possibility or without

possibility. When actuality is with possibility, the form is in matter. When actuality is without possibility, it is a certain Necessity. For what is without possibility is not changeable or mutable in any way because, as we have said, possibility is nothing other than changeability or mutability.

30. Truly then actuality without possibility is Necessity because it is form without matter. And therefore it is eternal. Likewise that which is neither matter nor from matter nor in matter rests on no principle except itself. Thus since form without matter is eternal, that form is God since God is eternal.

And because nothing can be accidental to a form, God who is form without matter, is unchanging and one. And if God is one, God is unity, because there are as many predicates as the subjects allow. For just as being is predicated substantively of God and participatively of creatures, as we said above, so the one proposition articulated about God signifies the divine substance which is unity. This implies a participation in unity by creatures.[24] Whence Boethius in another place shows that oneness and being and God are equal.[25]

31. While he is most skillfully examining the aforesaid subtlety concerning actuality and possibility in his *Liber Perihermenias,* Aristotle uses such a division to propose that a certain actuality exists with possibility, another actuality is nothing other than possibility alone, and a third is an actuality without possibility. I think we have spoken about form and matter as much as is necessary for the present discussion.[26]

32. So finally let us speak about the Trinity of persons and the generation of the Son from the Father and the procession of the Holy Spirit from both, as much as the divine light has found worthy to infuse into our mind, not because we are confident that we can attain a complete understanding of generation and procession—for we believe this to be impossible for a man—but so that we might contribute something to the defense of the Catholic position in the disputation against the heretics or the Jews, who so obstinately adhere to the unity of the divinity that they entirely deny the Trinity of persons.

33. Earlier it was made clear, I think, that God is unchanging and one. Whence it was concluded that God is unity. Indeed this word "unity" stated about God reveals not a quantity but the divine essence. If, however, God is said to be one, the suspicion of participation in unity can be raised by those who deny that such things are predicated in

such a way as the subject allows. Therefore if we would speak more correctly theologically, God is said to be "unity" rather than "one."

34. "This unity, therefore, generates at once an equality from itself.[27] For unity at once is nothing other than unity. But unity is an equality of unity. Therefore unity generates at once an equality of unity so that the same thing is unity and equality of unity, namely unity. This unity, therefore, is the Father because he generates; it is also the Son who is generated. Therefore the Father and the Son are one and the same. However the Father is not the Son nor the Son the Father for unity is not generated because it generates, nor is unity generating in that it is generated.

35. "And because the wisdom of the Father is the Son of the Father, it remains that the wisdom of God is the equality of unity and the integrity of being because," as was shown before, the equality of unity has been generated by unity, as the Son is said to be of the Father. "And by this phrase I think nothing could more truly be said than that the wisdom of God sets the manner and the term on all things. For in things there is nothing higher or lower other than what the wisdom of God comprehends." Whence above we called the form of the body flowing from the maker-form "equality and perfection," which imitates the first form itself inasmuch as it can.[28]

36. Since therefore it was clarified that the wisdom of God is the equality of being, it ought not to be forgotten that in the Letter to the Hebrews, the Apostle calls the Son "the image of the substance of the Father," for the reason that the Son, that is, the unity generated from unity, is the equality of being. For it is from the power of equality that one thing is configured to another thing and represents it through that image.

For example: if somehow you wanted to represent in a picture Abraham with his knife raised preparing to kill his own son by divine command, it is necessary that you strive to draw their individual members, that is, faces, hands, and feet, which you recognize to have been Abraham's and Isaac's, so that they can be illustrated in the same number and quantity.[29] Otherwise you will not represent very well what you want through the images. "Therefore the Apostle rightly calls the Son the image of the substance of the Father clearly because the Son, as we said, is the equality of being.

37. "Or he calls the Son the image of the substance of the Father because unity is the substance of the Father. But unity at once, al-

though not in operation or act, nevertheless is by power and nature the primal tetragon. For just as halves are made by twos and quarters by fours, unity at once constitutes a tetragon by arithmetical reasoning and also brings about the primal tetragon in nature."[30] Just as two times two drawn on a plane presents twoness on every side of a four-sided figure, so unity at once placed on a plane, divided into four parts, presents a unity on every side.[31]

38. The Apostle then perhaps calls the Son the image of the Father because the image of a multiple unity through its denomination, that is, unity at once, retains some shadow of likeness to divine generation. Whence even the Psalmist says: "God spoke once," that is, he brought forth from himself the Word at once, that is, from eternity. So also the Spanish Sybil, designating by the name "tetragon" the Son of the Father, says: "When you will arrive at the side of the eternal fixed tetragon and to the side of the eternal standing tetragons." She rightly attributes the primal tetragon in nature to the Son because the image of any tetragon is judged to be more perfect because of its equal sides. For this equality is identity.[32]

39. Therefore, having generated the equality of unity from unity at once, which is the Father, they are conjoined by a certain love: "unity loves the equality and equality the unity." This can be shown through the contrariety in natural things. "For everything that is exists because it is one." If something is separated into a plurality of parts, it immediately falls to its destruction. From this, then, it is clear that the division of its parts is odious to it.

For nothing loves its own destruction in so far that it preserves its own nature. "But everything that is tends to being." Since, therefore, a plurality of parts is the cause of its destruction, a unity of those same things is for it the cause of its being. And so unity, which is the equality of being, is beloved by it, just as a plurality of division is odious.[33]

40. "For it is not from any other source that any living thing fears the dissolution of its body."[34] Therefore it can safely be concluded: if unity flees division, then it loves what is equal to it, that is, unity; unity and equality of being are conjoined in a mutual love. "This love and connection is neither generated nor generates, but proceeds from unity and the equality of unity, not from one of them but from both. For the love or connection is not of one of them alone. That love and connection, therefore, proceeding from unity and the equality of

unity, is the Holy Spirit, so that since the Father is unity and the Son the equality of being,[35] we believe the Holy Spirit to proceed from the Father and the Son." But since this love, who is the Holy Spirit, proceeds from both, this love is without doubt in both. Each of them, however, is one and the same God. Therefore the Holy Spirit is God and not another god apart from the Father and the Son. For in God there is nothing except God.

41. We have set forth these things about the Trinity of persons according as the Holy Spirit has enabled us to speak. Now at last let us return to explicating the text. We said above how "every being is from form."[36] For a being is not nor could it be from matter. A being exists indeed through form because "form is the perfection and integrity of a thing."[37]

Boethius reaffirms that there can be no being from matter but "from form" by introducing an example, saying that the statue is not a statue from the bronze matter but from the form impressed on the bronze. And he shows this again in another example, that bronze is not bronze from the earth but from a quality of bronze. Again this earth is not earth *kaka ton ylen,* which is translated "according to its dense mass," that is, unformed matter.[38] But rather earth is so called from its forms which are dryness and heaviness. And because his opening remarks are a progression from many similar things being applied particularly to universal things, he concludes from these universally that "no being" exists from matter but "from form."

42. So he adds that there is in the divine substance a dissimilitude to natural things because "the divine substance is form without matter and therefore is one and is its own essence. For all other things are not their own essence. Any one of them has its existence from those things out of which it exists, that is, from its parts. And it is this and that part, that is, its parts conjoined, but not this part or this part singularly, as when an earthly man is made from soul and body, he is soul *and* body. He is not either body alone or soul alone. Therefore his essence is not in a part."

43. It is clearly taught here that all natural things exist out of matter and form, but the divine substance is form alone and therefore cannot be set in matter because it is absolute Necessity. Since Necessity is absolute, it is immutable. For there are four modes of universality.[39] There is absolute Necessity, which is divine providence in which all things are enfolded. And it is called absolute because it owes its

essence to nothing else. For it is that divinity to which all other things owe that which they are.

44. "From this absolute Necessity there descends a necessity of connection or combination, since those things which are enfolded in absolute Necessity from eternity are administered in the continuity of time as if by the combination or causal connection."[40] For thus the causes of things in the known works of God are joined so that, if they were referred to the divine foreknowledge in the continuity of time which the Greeks called *hymarmene,* one necessity infers another, although that necessity is unknown to men.

45. For Martianus Felix Capella in his *Liber Nuptialis* does not ignore the variety of human lots hidden within the Divine Mind in the place where he says: "He took from the revolving orb the spheres descending from the robe of Hymarmene's unmoving breast," meaning by "the revolving orb" a concordance of causes which carry some things or which are carried by other things and by "the spheres" those consequences which the aforesaid connection of causes brings about. He understands those consequences descending from the divine disposition as coming "from the robe of Hymarmene's unmoving breast" because, until the consequences of things come forth in the world, men do not know why evil things are dispensed to the good and good things to the evil.[41]

46. The third mode of universality is absolute possibility, in which all things except the divine are possibly connected but nothing is explicitly actual. For just as in an egg all parts of the bird are enfolded and in one grain of corn there are connected stalks and chaff with an infinite number of grains capable of sprouting up from it, so in absolute possibility, that is, unformed matter, all connected things, except the divine, can be concealed until nature produces them in actuality. This possibility is aptly called "absolute" because it owes nothing to any form but is rather understood to be free from every law of actuality.

47. The fourth mode of universality is definite possibility, that is, the same matter but understood in another way. For in this all things except for the divine are not concealed from the sense or the imagination or the reason in subsisting actuality. Whence it is called "definite" because what any one thing may be in it can be understood definitely from its form. But because it has already been clarified that "the divine substance is a form without matter," so it can be

affirmed surely to be absolute necessity. For "therefore it is one simply and its own essence." Of course, as Martianus showed somewhere, it is "truth existing apart from non-existing things" because it is most foreign to any law of composition.[42]

48. Further "all other things" which exist in matter "are not their own essence," that is, they are composed or can be put together. For we can truly say of none of the things that are composite "this exists," since "its own parts" prohibit the truth of that statement because an individual thing composed of parts is its parts. I do not say this part or that taken singularly, but this and that taken at once.

Neither can any part be predicated truly as integral of the totality, although the bishop of Poitiers allows integral parts of the totality to be predicated singularly and separately, fashioning a falsehood for himself in logic or certainly badly understanding the principle which is "every genus of an integral part is predicated of its own totality." He well understands that the genus of the part is a quality of the part, but he applies it poorly. Indeed he so applied the aforesaid rule in the predication of integral parts that according to it he predicated a part of the entirety with a substantive word. For example, he would say "Socrates is his own head."[43]

49. But really if he had wanted to make this predication through adjectival words, the aforesaid rule would not be broken because the quality of integral parts can be predicated of the whole with adjectival words, such as "Socrates is headed."

Integral parts can never be predicated with substantive nouns, just as the philosopher taught with the clearest example: "As when an earthly man is composed of soul and body, he is body and soul. For he is neither body alone nor soul alone." And immediately he concludes: "Therefore in a part," that is, a part of the connection of parts producing his totality, "he is not what he is," that is, he is not a simple thing.

50. The scholar Gilbert, bishop of Poitiers, introduces dark obscurity with great circumlocution into this most lucid passage.[44] He produces something so frivolous and in such convoluted words that one might believe that a certain integral part is predicated of the totality through itself alone and as our comedian Terence says: "Understanding, he causes no one to understand himself."[45] But I think that only a philosopher would have used a thesis to strain the meaning of the noun in this passage. For a thesis, as Aristotle writes in his *De*

topicis, is an unusual opinion of someone well known in philosophy.[46]

51. But now let us attend to what follows: "That, however, which does not consist of this and that, but only of this, truly is that which it is. And it is most beautiful and most secure because it depends on nothing else. Therefore this is truly one in which there is no number nor anything else other than that which it is."

52. After he has separated pure simplicity from natural and composite things, because a single thing is a plurality of composites, he attributes the purest simplicity to that being because it is recognized to be the most separated from something composed of parts. And whatever that highest being may be, he teaches that it is "the most beautiful" of all things since it conferred its being on the contraries of a world machine, ordering it beautifully and rationally. By its universality it is necessarily more beautiful. And because it contains no diversity of parts, it also is truly "the most secure" because it fears no dissolution of its parts.

53. For whatever contains in itself the cause of its composition, it retains in itself, while it exists, the cause of its natural dissolution. Therefore he has rightly said: "What is not from this and this, but is only this," that is, what is not joined out of parts but is truly simple is "truly that which it is" because they cannot predicate about it something separate that is part of it nor many things conjoined that are parts of it. For indeed there are none. Also the same thing is "most beautiful" because its form is whole. And it is "most secure because it depends on nothing else," that is, it is neither matter nor from matter nor in matter.

54. And for that reason it is truly one because it has "no number" of parts, no variety of accidents, and nothing "else in it other than that which it is. Nor can it become a subject. For it is form. Forms cannot be subjects. For although certain forms are subjects for accidents, as humanity, it does not receive an accident because it exists, but because matter is subjected to it."

55. He sets forth with this clear argument that the highest being is truly one and that no number of parts can be found in it from nature, namely, that the highest being is form and therefore cannot be subject to any variety because it is the common cause of forms. For insofar as there are forms, they can be subjects of no accidents because, although certain forms as humanity are seen to be subject to

accidents, as a man is white and tall and wise, in no way nevertheless are these accidents present from the nature of form but from
the property of matter.

56. Because matter and form are conjoined into one actuality—for
nature does not produce form without matter nor matter without
form—"this humanity" is seen to be subject to any accident. And
this is what he says: "For when the matter subject to humanity receives any accident, humanity itself seems to receive it."

He teaches that an aptitude of this manner of receiving accidents
by that form which is entirely without matter to be most foreign to it
because that form, as has been said, cannot exist in matter. For if it
could, it would not be said to be truly form but an image of a form.
And this is what he adds: "For form which exists without matter
cannot be a subject nor inhere in matter. For it would not be form,
but its image."

57. There follows: "For out of those forms which exist apart from matter
have come those forms which exist in matter and produce a body.
For we misname those things which exist in bodies in calling them
'forms' when they are images. For they resemble those forms which
are not constituted in matter."

58. Here the bishop of Poitiers calls forms which exist apart from matter "genuine substances," namely fire, air, water, and earth. Clearly
these are not those forms which have a mutual conjoining in *hyle,*
but rather which he labels as forms on account of matter and intel-
ligible species.[47] Between these forms and the aforesaid four substances, Plato assigns such a condition that they have a mutual conjoining in *hyle* as can be had between two circles, one of which is
drawn in the dust and the other in the mind. But substances of
this kind do not at all seem to exist apart from matter since they certainly exist out of matter and archtypical species.

59. Our teachers, however, call forms "which exist apart from matter"
idea which have existed in the Divine Mind from eternity and from
which those sensible things are produced. The outpouring of these
things is necessary if it is referred to the divine foreknowledge. But
if it is considered in itself, it is free and absolute in the same manner
that, as Boethius says in the fifth book of *De consolatione philosophiae,* each thing which lies open to the senses is universal if it
refers to reason, but singular if it is considered in itself.[48]

60. Let no one be disturbed here that the philosopher has used a plural
number when he said: "From those forms which are apart from

matter," as if one must believe in a diversity of forms in the Divinity. For it is not because there is a plurality of forms in God—in whom all things are one—that he speaks in the plural of "forms," but, because the form of divinity is one and its essence dispersed in all natural things, it shines forth in many subjects. It is for this reason that he says "from these forms which exist apart from matter," not from this form. Indeed just as the face of one man seems to be multiple because of its reflection in many mirrors, so also the Divine Form, though it is simple and one, is called a multiple more than a plurality of those things to which it gives being. Wherefore he says: "From these forms which exist apart from matter come those forms which are in matter," because, as has been said before, it was necessary for these things to come forth in matter if they referred to those things which were constituted in the Divine Mind from eternity.

61. Or if it pleases us we may understand the genuine forms "which exist apart from matter" to be those four substances that exist out of *hyle* and archtypical species. So "those forms which exist in matter" are well said to have come from these as from causes pre-existing before the conjoining.

According to another sense, those "forms which exist apart from matter" are aptly said to produce "a body" because that is sure to happen by reason of the aforesaid necessity and the available matter. And "those forms which exist in bodies" ought rightly to be called not forms but "images" of forms because they have descended by reason from the *idea* of the Divine Mind or from those four most pure substances and thus have degenerated from those preceding them. Certainly when we call these "forms," we misuse the name because they have nothing of form apart from an imaged likeness of form.

62. There follows: "There is no diversity in it, no plurality from diversity, no multitude from accidents and for that reason no number." If we remember what was said earlier, we cannot be misled by these words because we have shown above that God is simple form.[49] Whence Boethius infers as a consequence that no diversity of any kind can exist in God.

63. There are four modes of diversity. Now one kind of diversity is from the different definitions of such things which are found to be different in the same actuality: as substance and any of its qualities which, although they are different by reason of substance, are not, however, plural in number.[50]

64. Another kind of diversity is of those things which are segregated by different substantialities, as a man and a lion. A third kind of diversity is of those things which are separated only by accidents, as Plato and Aristotle. And the fourth diversity is only that one thing is not another. In this kind of diversity alone do the persons differ in God.

65. Since, therefore, he says: "there is no diversity in God," he has removed that kind of diversity from God which constitutes a diversity of definitions: as of a substance and any of its qualities. Having also said: "there is no plurality from the diversity," he has separated that kind of diversity from the divinity which produces a dissimilitude of substantial differences. Finally when he said: "there is no multitude from accidents," he removed that manner of diversity from the divinity which a variety of accidents alone causes, as is known to be between Aristotle and Plato.

66. But he does not remove from among the persons the fourth manner of diversity, by which alone one thing is not another, because, as has been said, there is only that diversity among the three persons that one is not another. And therefore in the divinity there is no number because the diversity of definitions and the variety of substantial differences and of accidents are foreign to it.

III

1.   Now let us see what follows: "Indeed God does not differ from God in any way.[1] For he cannot be separated either by accidents or by substantial differences placed in the subject. Indeed where there is no difference, there is not at all any plurality. Hence neither is there number. Therefore there is only unity."

That there is no number in God Boethius demonstrates with clear reason. For it is reasonable that God differs from God neither substantially nor accidentally. Moreover, "where there is no difference," there can be "no plurality" especially since plurality by necessity requires difference. There is in God, therefore, "only unity," that is, God is only one essence.

2.   For he says that God differs from God "in no way," that is, by no thing, that is, neither "by accidental nor substantial differences placed in the subject." This passage is explained differently by different people, such that some refer "being placed in the subject" only to accident. For accidents exist in a subject. Further substantial differences are not in the subject because they are parts of the species which lead to its existence. Whence Aristotle in *Praedicamentorum Liber* defines accident in this way: "I say something exists in the subject which, since it does not exist in something as one of its parts, cannot possibly exist without that in which it exists."[2]

3.   This Aristotelian definition, therefore, does not allow substantial differences to exist in a subject. Indeed Aristotle himself in the same book of *Praedicamentorum Liber* clearly states that to inhere in differences is not to exist in the subject.[3] Others also argue that substantial differences are placed in the subject but do not, however, exist in the subject, for they exist in subjects by mediating genera which collect into a species, as rationality is placed in the subject Socrates by the mediant man. Or substantial differences are placed in the subject, that is, they are joined together in what is inferior.[4] And thus "subject" can be taken equivocally, in one way because of accidents, in another because of differences.

4.   Because, therefore, God does not differ from God either substantially or accidentally, rightly is it asserted that there is only unity in him. To this assertion another appropriate cause is added as if as a

response to a silent objection: "For though God is repeated three times when he is called the Father and the Son and the Holy Spirit, unless we are thinking of numerable things and not of number itself, then the three units do not make a plurality of number in him since they are the same. For the repetition of units makes number. However in that number which consists of numerable things, the repetition of units and plurality does not in the least produce a numerical diversity of the numerable things."

5. The obscurity of this passage admonishes us to review a bit more something about number because different people have explained this passage variously in their expositions. There are those who say that there is only one unity and although in other authorities many units are regarded as many subjects which a single unity informs, they do not affirm that the cause for unity itself is thus found. Others attribute single units to single subjects, thinking it impossible for single things to be what they are by one unity. It is not good counsel for us to attempt to settle this quarrel for it will be sufficient for our perplexity in explaining this obscurity to avoid fault even if we cannot merit praise.[5]

6. For next the philosopher is about to say that number is twofold. Whence one must skillfully explore whether in this duality of number he wants to understand two species of number.[6] Now there are those to whom this is acceptable. And they say there is one unit by which a thing is called "one" and another by which it is one thing.

They likewise call one duality two units by which two things are numbered, and another duality two units by which the two are two things. And so on through the series of cardinal numbers. Whence St. Augustine in his *De Musica* divides number into corporeal and incorporeal. And I think he wished the corporeal to be the number by which things are however many they are, the incorporeal that by which things are counted however many they are.[7]

7. And indeed that number by which things are however many they are occurs in substances because something's one unity is in its substance as in its foundation. That number by which things are counted however many they are by their own singular unities adds singularly to the things enlarged by counting, just as the breath of a syllable is enlarged singularly in units to become a subject of the number by which we count. The numbers which are in numerable things, three or however many more repeated units there are, do not

necessarily make a plural number in things. But in counting numbers, many units repeated make a plural number.

8. However many units are gathered here, that many may become breaths of syllables extended into a word. Whence this number is called "a collection of units." But that number which is in things, as I say, is a multitude of ones. This number by which we count is sometimes about one thing repeated in number, sometimes about things discrete in number. About a thing one in number as when it is said: "This thing is one sword, this thing is one brand, this thing is one blade." Note that by repeating thrice the unit about the same thing I have not driven the subject into plurality. I make a unity into a plurality only by adding to the unity according to the threefold repetition of the number by which I counted.[8]

9. It is clear that this same number can be repeated about discrete things. Indeed when we say: "Socrates is one man, Plato is one man, Cicero is one man," this threefold repetition of unity, however, in no way constitutes a unity by adding to the unity according to the number by which we count. Indeed the number which is in things, by which doubtless things are however many they are, has been made clear by the diversity of the three men whom I have numbered. This thought about the two kinds of number seems to have been sufficiently explored. For since something is not called one unless there are two, a philosopher can be accused of speaking ineptly if concerning the same number he pronounces it both one thing and another.

10. There are some who say that there is no such division of number in species but there is the same number "which is in things and by which we count." And thus it is called one thing and another by the philosopher for there is one reason for number to be inherent in things and another to number things by a number. This opinion seems in no way to need refutation because we often divide the same thing as if into many because it is subject to diverse considerations either of reason or of imagination or of sense, as we can call a man a secondary substance and a primary substance. That is primary, Aristotle says, "and is properly and principally and most often called a substance which is neither in a subject nor said about a subject, as some man or some horse."[9]

11. Further intuition judges likewise that a man can be called a secondary substance. As Boethius says somewhere when he is giving

his own definition for man, "a man is a rational mortal animal." The notion itself is universal. For no one is unaware that man also has sense and imagination.[10]

Therefore, it can be properly and sufficiently held for things themselves to be counted by the same number that is in things, although the philosopher will say there is one number that is in things and another by which we count those same things. Indeed in the *Arithmetica* he does not make any mention of this duality of number. But he does divide number itself into even and odd as into the fullest species of number.[11]

12.   Because St. Augustine divides number into corporeal and incorporeal, however, this division about number as it is in things and as it is abstracted from things can be true. This appears in the category of quantity as follows: "There are things whose parts have no place: time, number, speech. For when we say 'one,' having said the number alone but not numbering anything corporeal, we do not see either its right or its left. Certainly it is not possible to point out the placement of its parts since it exists in a word."[12]

13.   It seems clear here that Augustine wants the incorporeal to be the number which proceeds serially in numbering things in the way that a boy is taught to count. And this number is abstracted and separate from every subject. I cannot recollect, however, if Augustine understood it thus in *De Musica*.[13] I do recall reading that number was corporeal and incorporeal. But whether he wanted that understood about number "which is in things and by which we count things" or about number inabstract and abstract, I do not remember clearly enough.[14]

14.   With this preview of these points, I hope that I have prepared an easier transition to this difficult matter for the readers, should there be any. And so let us return to the words of the text: "For though God is repeated three times when he is called the Father and the Son and the Holy Spirit," and so forth.

The previous discussion taught that by necessary reason there is only unity in God. Since, however, it seemed possible to object that a threefold repetition of the Deity made a plurality of gods, the philosopher himself set forth why it could not be so, saying that "the three units do not make a plurality of number because they are the same," that is, the unity repeated thrice does not make a plural number of the Deity in its essence because there is nothing other than the one Deity, although there might seem to be three by the threefold repetition.

15. And he proves this to be true in regard to the numbering of natural things when he says: "If we think about numerable things and not about number itself," that is, if while making a careful examination we investigate the subject itself which subsists in number, even though unity is predicated thrice about it, it is not, however, brought into plurality. Whence in what follows he adds two examples: the first, synonym, we will discuss immediately; the second is the univocal.[15]

16. In certain manuscripts, we read this: "Three unities do not make a plurality of number in that which exists itself." This reading can be explained thusly. One number is said to be "in that which exists itself," namely, the number of things. For every multitude of things exists. But another number is produced "in that which exists itself" and this is only a counting number. The passage which follows supports this reading and explanation well and connects smoothly to the passage which says: "If we think about numerable things and not about number itself. . . ."

17. That he does indeed use this phrase "not about number itself" has already been made clear in large part where I demonstrated that the number "by which we count" produced plurality because "in that case," that is, by the numbers which count things, "the repetition of units does make a number," that is, a plurality.[16] Indeed when I say; "this thing is one sword, this thing is one brand, this thing is one blade," through the threefold repetition by adding unit to unit I did produce a plurality of the numbers which count things, but I did not produce multiple subjects.

18. And so he adds: "In that number which consists in numerable things," that is, in things subject to number itself, "the repetition of units and the plurality do not in the least make a numerical diversity of the numbered things." Because, however, the philosopher himself admonishes us to turn to an inspection of this subtlety regarding "numerable things and not number itself," he sets forth next the duality of number about which the lesson investigates, saying: "For number is twofold: one by which we number, another which consists in numerable things."

19. If I were to repeat again those things which I said about the duality of number, I would do nothing except labor in vain. Nevertheless it

should not annoy me or anyone else to repeat that when numbering something I say, "one, two," and so forth, proceeding according to the series of number, that number is implied which is in things. But with these nouns, "unity, duality," the number by which we count ought to be understood. Nevertheless these words, namely "unity" and "one," signify principally the same thing.

20.　And this is what the philosopher says: "For indeed one is a thing; unity that by which we call something one. Again twos are in things," that is, what are called two are two things "as two men or rocks." Duality is that to which two things are subjected.

But we must carefully consider here what this means since "duality" is said to be "nothing" because duality is twice unity. We cannot deny that unity is something. But something can adhere or inhere in two things because there are two numerable things in the two. This is the case with two men in whom something can inhere as whiteness or sanity, or to whom something can adhere as paternity and sonship.

21.　Duality is thus nothing to which something can adhere or inhere. For duality cannot inhere in duality or in two things nor can it adhere to whiteness or sanity or any of the other accidents. I speak, however, of natural things because certain accidents occur only from the mode of considering them, such as generality and speciality, while other natural accidents of the natural world are bestowed because nature brings them forth in their subjects, such as white and black. For just as qualities are not themselves qualities but the causes of qualities, so quantities are not themselves quantities but the causes of quantities. Wherefore neither unity nor duality can properly be called "one."

22.　Nevertheless "one unity" and "one duality" can be spoken of by using a word which describes the effect of a cause figuratively, as when death is called "pallid" because it produces paleness. Thus "one unity" and "one duality" can be spoken of by using that figure of speech by which a word of an effect is given to a cause.[17] I do not know how duality ought to be called "one" other than figuratively since twice unity cannot be called "one" in any rational sense, and duality, moreover, could not exist except as twice unity. And thus the philosopher: "Duality is nothing except the duality by which two men or rocks become two," that is, are counted.

23.　Or if you prefer: "Duality" is "nothing," so that the missing word "is" should be supplied: such as is to be understood of the aforesaid, "there are two men or two rocks." "And in the same way for the rest" because just as one thing is subject to unity, unity indeed is that by which one is counted, and again just as there are two things subject to duality, duality is that by which twos are counted, so we are able to calculate about the remaining numbers.

24. There follows: "Therefore in the number by which we count the repetition of units makes a plurality. In the number of things the repetition of units does not make a plurality." The philosopher has already taught that there is no plurality of things in the threefold unity of number which is repeated of one thing. But in the number by which we count there is produced a plurality from the repetition of units. Whence he offers an example of the duality of number which we explained. And so he concludes surely what he proposed above, that is, "in the number by which we count" a repetition "of units produces plurality; but in the number in things there is in no way a plurality arising from the repetition of units."

25. In proof of this truth he offers a most lucid illustration: "As if I were to say of the same thing, one sword, one brand, one blade. For one sword can be recognized in so many words since this is more the re-iteration of a unity, not a numbering. Or if we said: blade, brand, sword, there is the repetition of the same thing, not a counting of different things." The reasoning behind this illustration has been explained sufficiently above. The philosopher here elucidates his point further when he shows that the reiteration in the unity of the same thing repeated three times is a counting number, not the counting of different things, as has been shown above.

26. Indeed he beautifully and fittingly confirms the very truth of this assertion with his example: "Or if we said: blade, brand, sword." For these three names of one thing have not multiplied the thing itself. Moreover the threefold extension of names produces the number "by which we count." But he adds another more fitting example to the first because in the first illustration the identity of the thing and the diversity of the words might seem to upset its appropriateness with regard to the Divinity since the Father and the Son and the Holy Spirit are one Deity and one noun is thrice repeated about them when we say "the Father is God, the Son is God, the Holy Spirit is God," wherein there is an identity of both name and substance univocally. His second example is:

27. "Or if I should say: 'sun, sun, sun,' I would not make three suns but I would have spoken several times about one thing." From this he

can conclude more securely, having exposed openly that which lay hidden in the question that "if God is predicated about the Father and the Son and the Holy Spirit, the threefold predication does not make a number." To this one may add, of gods. "This is a threat to those," namely the Arians, "as has been said, who make a distinction of merits among them," specifically of greatness. For they perversely think that the Father is greater than the Son, and the Son greater than the Holy Spirit. Catholics are indeed far removed from this error since they assign no diversity among the persons except that one is not the other. For the persons differ neither in genus nor in species nor in number.

28.   For Catholics, because they consider the Divine Form itself as it is in itself, that is, simple and without diversity, hold it as such and do not think it other than what it simply and truly is. So they do not falsely allege the Father to be of more majesty or merit than the Son, or the Son than the Holy Spirit. For this reason, therefore, "for those," namely the Catholics, who look into the truth of the divine *ousia* in this way, this is not seen as producing "an enumeration" of divine things "when it is said: the Father is God, the Son is God, the Holy Spirit is God," but rather a repetition of one and the same Deity about three persons.

29.   This is indeed what the philosopher puts forth: "To Catholics, who allow no differences in the Divinity and hold that form to be as it is and rightly thinking that it is not other than it is, it appears to be a repetition of the same thing rather than an enumeration of a diversity when it is said God the Father, God the Son, and God the Holy Spirit." But because he introduced two examples above, one of synonyms and the other of univocals, in order to assert the unity of the three persons, he adapts both fittingly to the subject matter when he adds: "And this Trinity is one God as the blade and the brand and the sword are one, as the sun, the sun, and the sun are one sun."

30.   So immediately he adds the reason for his introduction of these examples as well as a clarification of them: "But, meanwhile, let this be enough for my meaning and the proof by which I have shown that not every repetition of units produces number and plurality." This is as if he were to say: Whatever I wanted to confirm through the introduction of examples, this I intended by their introduction, that it may be truly understood that "not every repetition of units" produces a plurality of numerable things.

31.   Because the philosopher offered the example about the blade and
        the sword, which are synonyms, into his argument and thus the
        names of divine persons might be seen by someone to be synonyms,
        he skillfully eliminates this possibility when he adds: "But it is not
        truly said Father and Son and Holy Spirit as if they were synonyms."
        And finally he introduces this reason: "For the brand and the blade
        are one and the same thing."

        But the explanation is far different in regard to the names of di-
        vine persons because since the substance is the same for this sword
        and this brand and this blade, that which is this sword is this blade
        and this brand. Of the three persons, however, that is, the Father,
        the Son, and the Holy Spirit, although there is the same *ousia,* he
        who is the Father is not the Son or the Holy Spirit. Nor is he who
        is the Son the Holy Spirit or the Father. But what the Father is, so is
        the Son and the Holy Spirit. And what the Son and the Holy Spirit
        is, the Father is. Whence that outstanding poet Sedulius versified in
        this way:

        > Not because who the highest Father is,
        >   this the Son is,
        > But because what the highest Father is,
        >   that the Son is.[18]

32.   This, therefore, is what he says: "The Father and the Son and the
        Holy Spirit are the same but not identical." "In this matter" the
        philosopher admonishes and exhorts us to be cautious and atten-
        tive when he writes: "In this matter one must reflect for a while."
        Here he immediately introduces the dispute of the Catholics and
        the heretics about the three persons in the Deity, showing how the
        heretics make false inferences from the true belief of the Catholics.
        For when the heretics ask the Catholics whether "The same one
        who is the Son is the Father," the Catholics respond, "Certainly not."

33.   And likewise when the heretics ask the Catholics whether "The one
        is the same as the other," the true Catholic response is, "Certainly
        the one is not the same as the other." So it is from Catholic beliefs
        of this kind that the heretics conclude not only that which could
        be inferred from what is conceded, that "thus there is not com-
        plete indifference among them," but also what seems to follow nec-
        essarily from these concessions when they say "wherefore number

enters in," that is, the three persons differ in number among themselves.

34. Now the philosopher shows what kind of number the heretics want there to be among the persons, specifically, such as there is among many subjects from the variety of accidents, has been explained above. This is, therefore, what he says: "Which number has been explained above to have occurred from the diversity of subjects." This, then, is what he concludes: "In this matter one must reflect for a while. For having been asked: Is the Father the same as the Son? They answer, 'Not at all.' Again, is one the same as the other? This is denied. Thus there is not complete indifference among them. Wherefore there enters in that number which, as has been explained above, occurs from the diversity of subjects."

35. The error of the bishop of Poitiers can be seen to have arisen from this passage when he asserts that the three persons are different in number even though the philosopher above plainly refutes this error where he says: "But in things diverse by number the variety of accidents makes difference." And likewise a little later: "Therefore there is no diversity in God, no plurality from diversity, no multitude from accidents, and therefore neither is there number. God does not in any way differ from God nor is he separated by accidental or substantial differences placed in the subject. Wherefore there is no differentiation, no plurality of any kind, wherefore neither is there number. Thus there is only unity."

36. See how he straightforwardly refutes the error of the bishop of Poitiers since nothing can differ in number which a dissimilitude of accidents does not vary.[19] And likewise if God differs in no way from God, then since the Father is God, he differs in no way from God the Son and in no way from God the Holy Spirit. And likewise the Son and the Holy Spirit, since they are God, differ in no way from God the Father. Therefore, the three persons do not differ among themselves in number. Because his book, repudiated and condemned in the Council of Rheims under Pope Eugenius on account of other errors, was removed from the reading list for scholars and monks, and because his error which I have just mentioned was not included among other heresies raised at the Council, it seems appropriate to me to recall here the words with which he wanted to interpret this very passage, lest anyone be able to say that I either rashly or jealously or even mendaciously find fault in a man of such renown.

37. Gilbert says: "To those asking Catholics whether 'the Father is the same as the Son,' the Catholics reply: Not at all is the Father the same as the Son. Again having asked the same Catholics whether one is the same as the other, I do not say other in the singularity of essence but in the property of one subsistence; this is denied by them. From this, therefore, it is clear that 'not in every matter is there indifference among them.' For although there is indifference among them in that by which they exist, that is, in the essence which is predicated about them, there is nevertheless difference among them through those things which cannot be said of one but which must be said of another. Wherefore, namely, according to their diversity there enters in a number of those things according to which they are so called, so that they, who are one by the singularity of one essence which is said of them, are plural in number by diverse properties which may not properly be affirmed of each one.

38. "It has been explained above which number results, namely, that which a dissimilitude of accidents makes, and this is proved from the diversity of subjects or you may say of subsistence or subsistences conforming substantially among themselves since we enter into numbering out of a plurality of natural things."

39. I am rather doubtful here whether I should speak or be silent. The philosopher, indeed the universal faith, removes accidents entirely from the Deity according to the exigency of the Divine Form. But that man, as I understand him, wants to vary the persons by accidents. Whence he dares to speak so as to introduce among the persons a number which is made from the dissimilitude of accidents. But since in this place his error is seen to be as obvious as it is reprehensible or rather perhaps he was laboring incorrectly to accommodate this passage to the views of the heretics, let us consider now what follows in Boethius.

40. For the philosopher says: "We shall consider briefly this matter if beforehand we examine how anything can be predicated about God." "In order to remove the aforementioned error of the heretics, he promised to say a few words about predication."[20] But before we attend to the words of the philosopher, we must set forth what a predicate is and what is proper to any one predicate, so that we may clearly see that the divine substance exceeds every law and rule of predicates.

IV

1. The same philosopher in his *Commentum super cathegorias Aristotilis* says that a predicate is "a kind of signification in words," calling "a kind of signification" the mode of signifying which occurs only through words themselves, whether of quiddity or quantity or quality or some other way. Others say that any thing predicable, whether of quiddity or quantity or quality or any other way, is a predicate. And although there may be many predicables of quiddity, there are not for that reason many predicates of substance. For any predicable of quiddity is nothing other than the one predicate of substance. And likewise all predicables of quiddity are the one predicate of substance.

2. And they confirm this by an analogy. They say that just as the word "man" or any noun is this part of speech, namely noun, and there are many such nouns, nevertheless this part of speech, noun, is not multiplied but remains only one part of speech because all nouns are one part of speech. This is because of the same mode of signifying that they have. So anything predicable of quiddity is one predicate of substance and all predicables of quiddity are the same predicate because of one and the same mode of predicating that they have. They want to philosophize similarly about other predicables which are predicated of quantity or quality or relation or some other mode of predication.

3. There are others who want a predicate to be the simple signification of any primary genus. And indeed any one of the most general ten primary genera taken in itself can be suitably so called. So it is named a "predicate" according to them inasmuch as it is signified by this word. However they say the most general can exist although it is signified by no word. Because they pay too little attention to the matter, they indifferently call it "a most general predicate" and "a predicate most general."[1]

4. It seems best to us to call "predicate" any primary notion with further notions added to itself in the order of predicating. For we acknowledge that the objects of notions, which no one would deny to be sensible as well as imaginable, exist neither in predicates nor from predicates, but are subject to predicates. It seems to us unnecessary

to consider those who constitute the predicates in words alone, since this view, compared with other proposed positions, rests on an emptiness with no philosophical authority except that by which Boethius in his *Commentum super praedicamenta Aristotilis*, while he was introducing the uneducated and neophytes according to their capacity, said that Aristotle's intention concerning the ten primary words was to treat the ten primary genera of things by significations.

5. But if they wanted to examine diligently the disposition of Saint Augustine in this matter, they would desist immediately from this frivolous and puerile sense, especially since Boethius in the same *Commentum* can be shown to have prepared that commentary only for beginners and those of limited capacity. While in the *Secundum Commentum,* which we believe is lost, he is thought to have expanded upon the opinion of Aristotle, or so many claim.

6. The following words of Saint Augustine in his *Cathegorias decem,* which he appropriated from Aristotle in such a way that he would not set his feet in Aristotle's footsteps on the journey, seem to agree with this lost work: "There is a question many are accustomed to ask concerning what it is that Aristotle wants to examine at the beginning of his treatise on the predicates. First, is it those things that exist? Or, second, those things that are perceived? Or, third, those things that are spoken? These are all things that nature produces. Those things are perceived whose images we form and build, seeing them in our minds. Those things are spoken which come from those things which have been impressed on the mind. Whatever one conceives in his mind he can declare afterwards in language."[2]

7. After he has supplied the evidence of Themistius, Saint Augustine immediately reveals the mind of Aristotle in the *Cathegoriarum Librum:* "But as Themistius, a learned philosopher of our time, would agree, Aristotle intended to treat those things which are perceived and which he called by the Greek noun *simenomema* or phantasies, that is, images of things resting in the mind."[3]

8. See how he supports with the authority of Themistius that Aristotle intended to treat in the predicates the notions of things even though he seems to produce a multifaceted treatise, dealing sometimes with those things that exist, sometimes with those things that are perceived, sometimes with those things that are spoken. What Saint Augustine calls "perceptions" others call "notions," others "passions of the mind," others *intellectus* or *intellecta.*

9.   Whence Cicero in his *Topica,* which he wrote for Gaius Trebanus, gives a description of notion that is consonant with the description of Saint Augustine. "A notion is a cognition of the mind made from the form impressed after perception."[4] Augustine indeed gave this definition of perception, which although we have already stated it we set it forth again since we want to show the similarity of the two descriptions: "Those things are perceived whose images we form and build upon seeing them in our minds."[5]

10.   Aristotle, however, more fittingly called them "passions of the mind" in the first chapter of the *Librum perihermenias* for the reason that the mind itself is understood to suffer and be affected in some way by the impressed forms. It was the custom of Master Hugh rather to call them *intellecta* for the reason that the word *intellectus* is used to mean many different things, since error would be more easily born in his hearers if he called it *intellectus.*[6]

11.   Since, as we have shown, Aristotle began his treatise on predicates concerning the notions of things, for this reason Augustine treated first the rational causes of those things that exist, then of those things that are spoken and with these as well of those things that are perceived. He adds: "But this must necessarily be mentioned since Aristotle proposed to talk about perceptions and about those things that exist and about those things that are spoken."

12.   He presents the necessity for this: "For perceptions arise from those things that exist which we have perceived by seeing. But a demonstration of perceptions fails unless they are demonstrated by the aid of those things which are spoken."[7]

13.   Because then Aristotle wanted especially to treat the notions of things in the predicates, thus we choose to call a predicate any notion with further notions added to it by the law of predication. We do not refute the remaining definitions of predicates since they are reasonable enough, except that one which makes them only aired sounds. Behold, I seem to have satisfactorily explained what a predicate is.

14.   Finally it seems opportune to say what belongs properly to any one of the predicates especially since, as has been said above, it is understood that the divine substance is beyond all substance and owes nothing to predicates.[8] For it would seem to be most proper for a substance that, since it is one and the same in number, it not be susceptible to contraries.

And so from this we understand that the Deity owes nothing to predication since God is a form in no way susceptible to accidents and therefore not to contraries.

15. Likewise God is nothing that this term "substance" can signify. For just as Boethius states in the *Commentum Categoriarum,* substance is understood in three ways. For either substance is unformed matter and it belongs to it to underlie forms and accidents, and in this way a substance is not received in a subject. Or it is a substantial difference and it belongs to it to constitute species with its genus, and in this way is not received in a subject. For nothing which is in a subject can constitute a species. Or it is composed of matter and form and it belongs to it to be a thing existing per se, and so also is not received in a subject.

16. Since, then, substance is spoke of in these three ways and thus this term "substance" has several significations, it is clear that God is nothing that this term "substance" signifies. Indeed he is not matter because he is simple form. Likewise he is not a substantial difference because he is not part of something conjoined, which every substantial difference is. Finally he is not composed of matter and form because he is simple form which is true form and that which exists. Therefore it is clear that God is beyond receiving substance in any one of the three modes.

17. It remains for me to teach how the Deity owes nothing to the predicate of quantity. Now it is the property of quantity to be called equal or unequal in itself. But every quantity is either continuous or discrete, either actual or potential. Moreover that is called spacious which is of continuous quantity and which receives a predication according to itself so that when we ask "how much?" the response is "this much." The questioner is made certain that it takes the predicate according to discrete quantity by a response of unity or plurality.

18. God, however, as the Psalmist testifies, is not quantified because "God is great and most praiseworthy and his greatness is without end." Therefore it cannot be known nor said that God is quantified. Also God is not a numerable unity because his substance is not a discrete quantity and according to the Psalmist "Our Lord is great and his great power and wisdom cannot be counted." Therefore, because the divine wisdom is the divine substance, it appears clear that there is no number in the Divinity.[9]

19. Likewise God is not in a place because, as Augustine attests, place is a space which any body can hold and occupy in its length, breadth, and height. Therefore, because God is not a body, he is not in a place. Moreover God himself is not a place because a body cannot be situated in him. Nor can he be perceived or recognized in a body. For as Saint Augustine says, "Place is perceived and known in a body but it must not at all be believed that he is a body."[10]

20. Again, God is not time nor is he temporal. He is not time because, as has been shown previously, he is a certain necessity and eternity. Also he is not temporal because every temporality is mutable. Every temporality and mutability necessarily descends from one immobile principle. This will be clear in this way. Let an adversary of this affirmation hold the opposite, saying that not every mutability descends from an immobile principle but there is something mutable which does not descend from one immobile principle.

21. Then I would respond. Something mutable is either made or not. If it is not made, then it is uncreated because if it is created, it is made. Therefore if it is not made, it is uncreated. If it is uncreated, it is eternal because, since it exists, if it is not eternal, it is created. Therefore if it is uncreated, it is eternal. The adversary, however, held something to be mutable but not made. Whence since he could fittingly conclude that something is eternal, it follows also that the same thing is immutable. Therefore it will be mutable and not mutable. This is a contradiction.

22. Since we have reduced this part of the hypothetical objection to absurdity, let us examine what can follow from the other part of the proposed contradiction. Now my adversary holds that something can be mutable but made. If, therefore, it is made, it is made mutable either by itself, which my adversary with his impious mouth would say, or by another. But if it is made by itself, it follows that it was coming to be at some time. Since, therefore, it was becoming, in accord with the authority of Aristotle, it was not, since what is being made something is not. But since it made itself, it was something, because if it were nothing it could not become itself. This conclusion then follows, that what became was not immutable since it came to be.

23. It is necessary that my adversary concede this because that thing, since it was mutable, was that mutable thing which was coming to be, because as my adversary admits the thing made itself. Therefore

it is clear that he who says that the same thing made itself is shown to be of an obstinate mind. Thus it remains that if it is made, it has been made not by itself but by another. Moreover if that by which something is made is eternal and immobile, I have found what I have been looking for. For since it is not eternal but made, my adversary's imprudence is manifested in the absurdity of the above impropriety, should he not blush to say that it is made by itself.

24.   But if he will say that something mutable is made by another mutable thing, I question again as above whether something by which something else is made has been made or not. If it is not made, my adversary will not evade the previous impossible conclusion, that is, the same thing being mutable and not mutable. For the same sequence of arguments will demonstrate this contradiction. However if it is made, but not by one immutable principle, it remains that it was made by something mutable and that thing likewise by another and thus there is no terminus of this descent of one thing from another.

25.   For an infinity of the kind found in this contradiction may not seem absurd to someone who might point out that Euclid demonstrates in his *Geometria* that since every line is composed of lines, then an infinity of lines may occur to someone carefully reflecting on the nature of line.[11] But we would reply that this is a small objection because although unknown to us there is nevertheless a fixed number of natural things.[12] For all things were made in number, weight, and measure by the Creating Form.[13] Number itself is from eternity the exemplar of created things in the mind of the Maker. But there is nothing in mathematics that prohibits the powers of the mind from extending to infinity and to reflect on anything as it is other than in actuality. For example, when we speak according to mathematical reasoning, we define a line as longitude without latitude although in the world of nature there is nothing that has length without width.

26.   And again although every lineal reality is bounded by a terminus, it is nevertheless possible to extend a line into infinity. Since, however, I have compelled my adversary to move ineptly to what is at the very least an absurdity, his deduction is what they call a "paradox." For Aristotle names the five kinds of improprieties in his *Sophistici Elenchi,* anyone of which, should my adversary be led into it, is liable to refutation. These are: "reproof, falsity, paradox, solecism, silliness."[14]

27. The proposition that one mutable thing could not come to be without an infinite number of things necessarily coming to be on account of this one seems to violate common sense. Therefore it is agreed that every mutable thing has descended from one immutable principle. That principle is the good of individual things in which it is present. For if that which is bad for things is what leads them to destruction, then that which confers being on them is necessarily the good of their being. And that principle is primary and good in itself. Therefore it is proved to be greater than those good things on which it confers being. Thus it is the highest of all good things and is called "God" in common discourse.[15]

28. Therefore they lie miserably and impiously who began recently to coin for God this most stupid heresy and allege falsely that these mutable things have come forth always from eternity and are not governed by God the Creator nor receive their beginning from God. And so they set up for themselves the impunity of all sin when they believe this impiety.[16] "Foolishness has said in her heart, there is no God."[17] Nevertheless the fool dares to put forth this heresy only under the obliqueness of insinuation, but he is not afraid of putting it forth to the ears of tender women and to laymen whom either age or enthusiasm can turn to this kind of emptiness.

29. Now because we believe it has been shown that every mutable thing has descended from one immutable principle and that principle without doubt is God, it is clearly evident that God is not temporal. Therefore, because there is in God neither so much nor so many (every quantity, as has been said, being either discrete or continuous, actual or potential), it follows that the property of quantity is alien to him, that is, to be called equal and unequal according to it. Therefore in the Divinity there is nothing owed to the predicate of quantity.

30. Neither does the Divinity owe anything to the predicate of quality. It is the property of quality according to itself to be called "similar" or "dissimilar" because quality is the like similitude of different things. Therefore because God is not a quality of different things— for he himself is the form of being and cannot exist in matter, as has been proved earlier[18]—nothing can be said to be "similar" or "dissimilar" according to him. Whence it clearly appears that the Divinity owes nothing to the predicate of quality.

31. The Divinity owes nothing also to the predicate of relation. Since being related depends always on another and since the being of the

Deity depends on nothing, it is clear that the Divinity owes nothing to the predicate of relation. And since it is the property of relation that, knowing one of the relatives by definition, the other can be definitely known and since the Divinity is unknowable, it is clear from this that the Divinity owes nothing to the predicate of relation.

32. Again the Divinity owes nothing to that predicate which is called "action" because to act is an action moving from one thing to another considered in that by which it moves. However earlier we proved from necessity that God is the immobile principle of all mutable things. Since he is immobile, he is unable to move from one thing into another. God, therefore, because he is immobile and ubiquitous, cannot move from one thing to another.

33. Likewise affection is an act moving from one thing into another considered in that which moves. Therefore the Deity, because it is immutable and ubiquitous, is shown to owe nothing to this predicate.

34. Where and when is being in a place and a time. Whence because it has been shown above that God is neither spatial nor temporal, it is clear that the Deity is not at all limited by these predicates.

35. Position is the placement of the parts of a thing in a place so that this part can be understood to be in front, that part behind, this on the right, that on the left, this above, that below. But the simplicity of the Divine Form cannot be circumscribed in a place since it lacks parts. Wherefore the Divinity is most free from the rule of this predicate.

36. Saint Augustine wrote that there are eight specific instances of the tenth predicate.[19] When he enumerates them, he is predisposed to understand that the Divinity owes nothing to that predicate called "state." The first instance is when we have something in the soul, as justice, chastity, or their contraries. The second is when we are said to have something in the body, as whiteness or blackness. The third comes from quantity, when we are said to have a length of three cubits or five feet. The fourth is when we are said to have something not on the whole body but on a part of it, as a ring on a finger or a stocking on a foot.

37. The fifth is when we are said to have something not on the body but around the body, as a cloak. The sixth is when are believed to have those parts of the body, as head, hands, feet. The seventh is when a vessel is said to have grain or wine in it. The eighth is what shows our possession or ownership when someone is said to have a building or a field.

38. Certainly many teachers dislike this term and argue it to be improperly used when a woman is said to have a husband or a man a wife, or a father a son, or a son a begetter. On account of this they assert that nothing is really had which one has in so having.[20] Now that you have reviewed these eight modes of having, you can clearly understand that the Deity is in no way susceptible to this predicate. For although the Deity seems to owe something to the first of the modes listed because in the Divine Mind powers and the forms of things are truly said to exist and thus the Divinity is asserted to have something in its mind as a man has justice and chastity in his mind, nevertheless it must be noted that whatever is in the Divine Mind is that very mind itself. But in the mind of man justice and chastity are understood to be accidents of the mind, not the mind itself.

39. Here it seems opportune to note that the Divinity surpasses the rule of predicates in such a way that it avoids every law of predication and subjugation. For if ever we should read in some scripture passage that the Deity is predicated about something or the Deity is subjected to something, this must be understood as a manner of speaking and we must allow literary license for these. Indeed to be predicated of something, as Boethius says, is to inhere in a thing.[21] But the Deity does not inhere in anything nor anything in it. Therefore it cannot be the subject of anything nor can anything be predicated of it.

40. We have a great abundance of arguments to demonstrate this truth. But because the truth can be revealed by one argument and we have already remained long enough on the predicates, let us return to the place where the philosopher says: "About this point we shall consider briefly" and what follows.

41. Already the philosopher has shown how stupid and false is the position of the heretics against the Catholics, namely that there is not indifference in every matter among the divine persons. And so he showed that according to the thinking of the heretics number comes between them. And so it is that he promises he will consider briefly whether the predicates are correctly introduced after he will have "first" shown "how anything may be predicated about God."

42. Therefore he says: "In all there are ten predicates which can be predicated universally about all things," that is, about the universe of all natural things, "namely substance, quality, quantity, relation, place, time, condition, situation, action, and affection." Now since

we have already spoken in this treatise about the predicates and their properties as we met them, we do not want to repeat here what we have said. But we do want to clarify the words which he adds following the list of the predicates.

43. For he says: "These, therefore, are such as their subjects allow." If a predicate can vary in natural things according to what is allowed of the predicates and that is not considered unusual, how much less unusual should it be considered in theological terms if the meanings of the predicates change in accord with their subject. Indeed in this proposition "an egg is an animal," although the word "animal" ought to be understood according to its natural meaning, nevertheless I say that here it is a proper name for the subject on account of the power and the nature of the possibility of its becoming an animal. For nothing else can possibly be made of the egg except an animal.

44. Therefore when some name of substance or quantity or quality or relation or any of the other predicates is predicated about God, no one should marvel if its meaning is transferred to some other sense. For words are invented for things according to the process of reason. The process of reason, however, is not sufficient to comprehend God. Only the power of *intellectibilitas* is, about which we spoke more fully earlier on.[22]

45. It is well said by the philosopher that predicates are such as the subjects allow. This he confirms by the following argument: "For one part of them is in the substantial predication of natural things and the other part is in the number of accidents. But when someone turns to predication in the Divinity, all the things that can be predicated are changed."

"In the predication of natural things" apart from God he says that part is substance, part is "in the number of accidents," for although God is substantial, he is nevertheless a substance not at all according to the three modes of the meaning of substance but is most truly and certainly a substance "beyond all substance," that is, the form of being.

46. Part of those things which are predicated as accidents, although they seem to be predicated about God accidentally, are not predicated adjectivally about God as about other subjects, but substantively, for when both substantive nouns and adjectives of whatever predicate are applied to divine predication, they all change their meanings.

Since the solution of the question must be found in those things which we call relation, he marks them as a certain manner of special predication saying that those things which are relation "cannot be predicated at all." It is not that they cannot be predicated of anything, but they cannot be predicated absolutely and per se but only in respect to another as when we say: "We admit this to you in every way," that is, without respect to anything and without any condition.

47. Augustine in his *Cathegorias* recalls this difference of predication: "Of those things which are predicated, some are predicated in substance, others outside of substance, some partly in substance, others partly outside of substance. Quality and quantity are predicated in substance, namely insofar as they inform and affect the subject in some way. All the others, excluding relation, are predicated outside substance."[23] Relations, according to Saint Augustine, as has been said, "are predicated partly according to the thing and partly outside the thing."

48. But the philosopher divides predication even more aptly. He says that any predication of substance, quantity, and quality which make that thing in which they are to be that which it is called happens according to the thing. The other seven, as will be made clear a little later, are predicated outside the thing. But every predication made about God is the same, because as the divine essence has no variation, so divine predication avoids every dissonance of multiformity.

49. Rightly, therefore, he says that all things change which can be predicated since in the divine predication they become different for "substance in God is not substance, but beyond all substance," that is, he is the entity itself from which substance descends. Likewise quantity "and quality and the others which can adhere in subjects" are completely changed in divine predication just as the philosopher says: "Likewise quality and the rest which can occur, for which I must add examples so that they may be further understood."

50. After he has shown that the predicates of substance and quality and the other accidents are changed when transferred to divine predication, he adds individual examples in order to make it clearer. He presents his first example of the predicate of substance in this manner: "For when we say 'God,' we seem to mean a certain substance but one which is beyond substance." This is as if he had more properly said that substance seems to be signified from a likeness to a quiddity capable of predication. When he says "the Father

is God," what is signified is not receptive of contraries but is an entity which is beyond all substance.

51. "When God is called just," a quality seems to be signified by the name "just." But that does not happen to God because his justice is his divinity which exceeds "all substance." This indeed is what he says: "While just is a certain quality, it is one that is not accidental but substantial, or rather beyond substantial. For indeed in God it is not one thing to be and another to be just, but it is the same thing for God to be and to be just."

52. Further when anyone predicates great or the greatest of God, he seems to predicate a divine quantity added on to God. But this is not so because the divine magnitude is the divine *ousia*. The philosopher sets forth the truth of this: "Likewise when great or greatest is said, we seem to signify a certain quantity but one which is that very identical substance which we said is beyond substance. For God it is the same to be and to be great."

53. He confirms that "in God it is the same to be and to be great" when he repeats an argument he used above, namely that God is a form to which nothing can adhere and therefore he is truly one and not at all a plurality. Since, therefore, God is great, he is nothing other than that which he is. For if he were one thing in his magnitude and another in his essence, he would not truly be one nor without variation.

The philosopher explains this point well in the following passage: "For it has been shown above concerning his form that he is this form and is truly one and lacks any plurality."

54. There follows: "But these predicates are such that they make that in which they are to be what it is called, diversely in natural things, but in God conjoined and united. For when we name a substance, as man or God, it is spoken of as if that about which it is predicated is a substance, as man or God is a substance. But there is a difference because man is not entirely himself 'a man' and thus is not a substance. What he is he owes to other things which are not man."[24]

55. The three predicates of substance, quantity, and quality are such that in natural things they make predicates and subjects the same things. So it is that since Socrates is a man, the matter of the predicated notion "man" and Socrates actually become in a certain way one and the same. And so these three predicates "make a thing to be what it is called," differently nevertheless in natural things and in

the Deity. For although white and two cubits tall are actually the same with regard to Socrates, they nevertheless function in different ways in him.

56. But in God all things are the same and have one state. For in him justice and magnitude, truth and goodness are the same. In man, however, justice is not the same as magnitude, because justice and magnitude differ as much from man by definition as substantial beings differ entirely among themselves.

But in God these are "conjoined and united" into one, as was said, because neither natural nor mathematical considerations can disunite them. Indeed divine justice is divine magnitude is divine mercy, although nevertheless divine justice damns sinners, this should not be ascribed either to magnitude or to mercy, as mercy forbears in such a way that it cannot be referred either to divine magnitude or to justice.

57. He intends to prove with additional examples that the three "predicates are such that they make that in which they are to be what it is called." For "when we say 'God is a substance' or 'man is a substance,'" substance is predicated of both such that the substance which is predicated of each subject is the same when it is said "man or God is a substance." But substance is predicated differently of God and man because "man is not complete," that is, man does not exist from himself. "And because of this he is not completely a substance" because such a substance, that is, man, is shown to owe his being to "others," namely to different parts or substantial differences.

58. God, however, owes to nothing that which he is because he exists from none other than himself. Whence the names of forms are not appropriate to those things which are material, as to man and lion and other natural things. For it cannot truly be said that Socrates is humanity or whiteness because his form is in the proper composition of his parts. And this you can easily see since we are accustomed to call things "unformed" when their parts are incongruously conjoined.

But because God is nothing other than form, reasonably and indeed rightly are the names of forms appropriate to him. Whence we can say universally and confidently that God is deity, justice, goodness, and truth.

59. We must now examine how the philosopher proves that man owes his being to "things other than are man," which reading one can find

in many manuscripts, since none of the substantive or integral parts of a man can truly be said to be man.[25] Thus animal is not the same as man but neither are rationality or mortality man.

60. Also it must be noted that all the substantial parts of man taken together are man. And no less the integral parts of man, if they are taken together, are man. The same author most cleverly affirms this in his *Commentum super Topica Ciceronis* when he inserts this in teaching something in the fourth book of the *Topica*.[26] But for the sake of brevity we are inclined not to reproduce these sources at the present time.

61. There follows: "But God is God himself. For he is nothing other than what he is. And for this reason God is himself." After he teaches that man in himself is not completely man, he most promptly removes any such assertion about the Divinity lest anyone be led by a stupid error to introduce the same thing in God, because "God is God himself" in that he is simple for neither different substantial parts nor any difference of parts can be present in simplicity. "And for this reason God is himself" complete, that is, "God is" from himself.

62. The predicate quality is applied differently in the predication of the Divinity and of natural things because this "quality" justice also makes those things in which it exists to be what they are called. So if we were to call Abel just, it is this quality justice which makes him just which he is truly said to be. Since we also hold that God is just, it is true that he is what he is called. However there is a difference between Abel being just and God being just because Abel is just because of what is not Abel, that is, justice. On the other hand, God is just for no other reason than he is God.

63. Whence you can say that Abel is one thing and just another, for Abel is not necessarily just because he is Abel. God is necessarily just because he is God for God is justice itself. This then is what Boethius adds after the example of the predicate of substance: "Again just, that is a quality, is so called as if it were identical to that about which it is said. If we say man is just and God is just, we hold man and God to be the same just things. But there is a difference, because man is one thing, just another. But God is the same as being just."

64. For the philosopher says "just, that is a quality" in the manner of Aristotle, who, as Augustine attests in his *Cathegorias*, used indifferently the word of the thing for the name of the quality and the name of the quality for the word of the thing.[27]

65. And now let us hear how the predicate of quantity makes that in which it is to be the same as what it is called. He says: "Man or God is called great in such a way as if man himself is great or God himself is great. But man is merely great. God exists as greatness itself." The predicate of individual things makes those things in which it is to be what they are called. Nevertheless it is different for Saul to be called great and God to be called great because Saul is not the magnitude by which he is great. But God is great for no other reason than that he is.

66. He then says that "those remaining" from the first three, that is, the seven most general predicates, are predicated about no thing. This I gather the philosopher states in comparison to the three predicates because, as has been shown, the three aforesaid make a thing to be something because they confer on it substantial or accidental being. The remaining seven do not have the power to inform a subject or to affect it in any way. Wherefore he says they are predicated about no thing and, as will be discussed in what follows, all of them are predicated outside of the thing.

67. Whence when he says: "The rest are predicated neither about God nor anything else," he does not delay in adding: "For place can be predicated about God or about man, about man, as he is in the forum, about God, as he is everywhere. But place is not predicated about its subject as if it were that thing itself. For man is not said to be in the forum in the same way as he is said to be white or tall, or as if surrounded and determined by some property by which he could be designated according to his very being. But this predicate only shows what is his situation to regard to other things."

68. You see how after he first said "the remaining seven can be predicated neither about God nor anything else" continuing on he asserts that place can be predicated about God or man. This indeed he could not have done unless he compared the predication of the seven to the force of substance, quality, and quantity. For as has been said, the informative force of these is such that they make a thing to be what is called.

69. But this predicate place, like the other six, is so predicated that "it is not predicated about its subject as if it were that thing itself." This is as if he had clearly said "place is predicated about man" not however as if the thing predicated and the subject constituted the same actuality. For indeed to predicate "being in the forum" about man is

to confer neither substantial nor accidental being upon him. For he is not in the forum in the same way that he is white or tall. For whiteness and height affect the subject itself. This cannot be said at all about place. Indeed place does not encompass a man with some inherent or notable property as whiteness does a man's head or his whole body because of which we are accustomed to call a man white.

70.　But neither does it set limits as a line does by which we measure the body of a man as being either two or three cubits tall. Therefore no place can "designate according to his very being" by the property which it may give to him because the circumscription of place is not in any part of a man, nor in the whole man as whiteness in the head or in the whole body makes him to be white and thus to be something. Nor does the circumscription of place exist in a man as a line or surface by which we are accustomed to measure the height and width of bodies. So thus Boethius finds no property of place by which a man himself may be "designated according to his being."

71.　"But by this predicate there is only shown what his situation is in relation to other things" because a thing is not said to be in a place in such a way that the place itself forms the thing. But by the predication of place it is stated that a man is enclosed in a place and circumscribed by the boundary lines, that is, "what his situation is to other things" more than "by some property by which" he may be "designated according to his being."

72.　"It is not the same with God. For that he is everywhere does not seem to mean that he is in every place, for he cannot at all be in a place, but that every place is present for him to occupy since he is not circumscribed by place. And therefore he is said to be not at all in a place because he is everywhere but not in any one place."

　　Boethius is saying that when a man is said to be in the forum, that is understood as a circumscription. But this predicate must be understood very differently about God. For he is not said to be everywhere in the sense that he is circumscribed or that he is limited to a place, for there is no capacity of place that can enclose him since as Boethius immediately says, "God is everywhere." This should not be taken to mean that God is enclosed by spatial lines in every place. And thus "he cannot at all be in a place."

73.　But he is said to be everywhere in this sense that "every place is present to him for him to occupy" without a limit. He says "for him to occupy" not because, as has been said, he can be encompassed or enclosed in any amount of place, but because there is no place in which the whole being of God can truly be found since "he is not susceptible to place" locally speaking. "And therefore he is said to be not at all" encompassed in a place because "he is everywhere" yet enclosed by no limits of any one place.

74. "Time is predicated in this same way, about man, 'he came yesterday' and about God, 'he always is.' Here again for man time is not predicated as if he were that very same thing [time] about which it was predicated that he came yesterday. But it is predicated according as time draws near to him. But what is said about God, 'he always is,' signifies one thing, as if he were in all the past, also is now in all the present, and will be in all the future. This also can be said, according to philosophers, about the heavens and certain immortal bodies."

75. Just as Boethius showed the predicate place to be predicated of man according to one reason and by another of God, so also he assigns the predicate time differently to creatures and to the Deity. Thus he declares that the two predicates have the same manner of predication when he says "time is predicated in the same way, about man, 'he came yesterday,' and about God, 'he always is.'" And indeed "about man having arrived yesterday" time is predicated so that the thing predicated is not the same actuality as the subject. Nor does such a predication declare man to be something. But this predication makes clear what happens to him in what time.

76. When it is said of God: "He always is," the "always" signifies that he is only one according to that usage by which the wise are accustomed to philosophize about natural things. For when one says "it always is" of certain natural things, the philosophers are accustomed to understand that phrase to mean "it was in all the past, is now in all the present, and will be in all the future" and to ascribe it to the world and the stars. And in this way when "it always is" is asserted about any one of the natural things, it is signified as being *semper est* [it always is] according to a succession of time in the same way as it appears to be signified about God.[28]

77. But this is not so, because God's *semper est* (he always is) is not a stretch of time but the present of immobile eternity. And so this is what he adds: "But this is not the case for God. For he is always because always for him is the present time." And immediately he

states the difference between the present of the divine things and of temporal things: "There is a great difference between the present for our reality which is 'now' and the reality of the Divinity. For our 'now' occurs as moving time and sempiternity. But the divine 'now' occurs permanently, unmoving and consistent in eternity. If you add *semper* to this noun *aeternitas* you will make it into a present which is that indefatigable conjoining and perpetual flowing which is sempiternity."

78. The difference of "present" between divine and temporal things has been made clear because the present of temporal things succeeds the past and comes before the future. And so "it occurs as moving time and sempiternity" which the planets and stars regulate. The divine present, ceaselessly permanent, moves by no change of antecedent or succession and "so it does not make sempiternity" but it remains and "conserves its eternity." If, however, you unite the power and signification of our "now," which adverb he introduces with the appellation of a noun when he says "if you add *semper* to this noun," with our *semper* in which there is found the antecedent and succession of time, you will discover the "perpetual flowing, which is called sempiternity" without interruption and also "a conjoining" without termination or laboring in perpetuity and therefore "indefatigable."[29]

79. There follows: "Again it is the same with condition and activity. For we say of a man: 'clothed,' 'he is running;' of God: 'possessing all things,' 'he rules.' Again in neither case is anything said of the subject's essence for each kind of predication is given about exterior matters."

That which he has already taught about place and time he says about the predications of activity and condition for when a man is said to be "clothed" or "running," neither condition, which is understood by "clothed," nor activity, which is understood by "running," confer anything essential on the man nor are they found in an identical actuality with that about which they are predicated, nor do they belong to the essence of a subject, nor do they inform the subject as qualities and quantities do.

80. Similarly when it is said of God: "Possessing all things, he rules," "he rules" refers to activity, "possessing" to condition. But the predication of both occurs outside the thing, just as those of place and time, and not according to the thing's essence. "All these are referred in a

certain way to something external." He says "in a certain way" lest anyone understand that those things are all the relations which may be referred in every way. Those "are referred," that is, they regard "something external," not informing its subject, as has been said, and are considered in other things apart from the subjects as if outside, just as "Socrates is in the forum" signifies that Socrates is in a place, not that a place is in Socrates and just as "today" signifies that Socrates is in time, not that time is in Socrates in the same way as whiteness and magnitude.

81.   Activity, which is an act of moving from one thing into another considered in that by which something moves, cannot in any way inform the agent since it is done by the agent. Will passivity, since it is an act moving from one thing into another considered as that which is moved, in any way inform the patient since it is the act of an agent? Can situation in some way inform a thing since the same form of Socrates remains whether he sits or lies down? Condition cannot be said to inform the thing because, whether Achilles has or does not have weapons, he is subject to no alteration by that condition.

82.   The philosopher will teach properly and briefly in what follows how it is that those predicates which are relation do not inform the subject. This, however, can all the more easily be understood because of those things which we have already discussed. Since one predication is according to the subject and another is outside it, Boethius introduces the signs by which their differences can be discerned. He says: "We can easily recognize the difference of this predication: 'Who man or God is' refers to the substance by which it is something, namely man or God. 'Who is just' refers to that quality by which there is something that is just. 'Who is great' refers to that quantity by which there is something that is great."

83.   He gathers into one the three predicates of substance, quantity, and quality. He teaches that they are predicated in such a way that they attribute something either substantial or accidental to their subjects and thus those subjects are something by these predicates. But he removes this mode from the other seven predicates and he confirms that this is the case by the introduction of examples. For when anyone says that someone is in the forum, as a man is, or everywhere, as God is, such predications are seen to refer to the predicate of place. Moreover those things which are subjected to the predicates cannot be understood to be something, just as it is Enoch's justice that is understood to be just when Enoch is called just.[30]

84. And when anyone says that someone is running or rules something or is now or is always, he is looking at the predicates of activity and time. Nevertheless the subjects are different from the things which are predicated, just as whoever is called "great" is great by magnitude. But the three aforesaid predicates make the thing in which they are to be what it is called, as whoever is called man or God regards the predicate of substance by which whoever is called a man or God is a man or God.

85. Should someone be called "just," as a man or God, this looks to the "quality" by which a man or God is just. Likewise should anyone be called "great," as a man or God, this may be seen to look to the predicate "quantity" by which a man or God is great.

    "For in the other predicates it is not the same. For whoever says that someone is in the forum or everywhere refers to the predicate 'place' but not to that by which he is something, in the same way that he is just by justice. Also when I say 'he runs' or 'he rules' or 'he is now' or 'he is always,' activity and time are referred to, if however that divine time can be designated by *semper*. But they do not refer to that by which something is in the same way that something is great by magnitude. And it is not necessary to inquire into situation and passivity regarding God. For they are not in him."

86. The text containing the examples of the three predicates of place, time, and activity has been explained sufficiently above, although he seems to have spoken with hesitation about the predicate time where he says: "If however that divine time can be designated by *semper*." It is as if he had appropriately said: when *semper* is said of God, it seems to look to the predicate of time. If, however, it has been said about God, it can refer to time since it designates the eternity of God rather than time.

87. And so perhaps the Divinity may seem to owe something to the other predicates, although, however, as has been explained, nothing is owed to them. Truly no one can be ambiguous about passivity and situation because the Divinity is impassive and exceeds every capacity of place.

88. There follows: "It is now clear what the difference is in predication, that some predicates point out the thing and others its circumstances. The former are predicated in such a way that they show the thing to be something, while the latter attach something not to its being but more externally. Therefore those which designate what something is may be called predicates according to the thing. When

they are said about subjected things, they are called accidents according to the thing. But when they are said about God, who is not a subject, that predication is called predication according to the substance of a thing."

89. After introducing examples of individual predicates, he says that the difference in predication is clear because the predicates of substance, quality, and quantity "point out the thing." For they make that in which they are to be what it is called. The other predications do not demonstrate the thing, as place and time which seem to demonstrate rather the circumstances, that is, the place and time which are sought in the performance of an action.

90. The rhetoricians divide *quando* [when] into time and occasion, the latter being an opportunity for doing or saying something which is brought forth in time.[31] An example of time is when someone says that Caesar conquered the Gauls in ten years. An example of occasion is when someone says that Catiline conspired against the Republic because at that time Pompey, waging war in Spain, summoned all the armies of Italy to himself.

The rhetoricians call that circumstance which is *ubi* [where] location, as Caesar was killed in the Capitoline.[32] Activity and passivity have some likeness to certain circumstances which are considered in things coherent with an action.[33] For example, circumstances can be divided into the sum of the deed, as the murder of a parent, which is similar to passion, and into "before the action," "during the action," and "after the action," which seem to cohere in the activity. "Before the action" is when someone is said to have raised his sword excitedly before the murder. "During the action" is when he was striking vehemently. "After the action" is when he secretly buried his parent.

91. When Boethius says certain of the predications point out the thing to be something, he asserts the others to be like circumstances of the thing and in a way to attach extrinsically to it something which is not the thing itself. This is on account of the likeness which these four predicates have with these circumstances or which are in things coherent with an action or are sought in the performance of an action. And after he demonstrates this, he sets out the proper division of predication, as we ourselves have done above, to wit, those predicates which point to that which a thing is, as quantity and quality, are predications according to the thing, while the others

may be called "predications outside the thing." When qualities and quantities are predicated about natural things as well as accidents in subjects, they are called "accidents according to the thing. But when predicated of God, who is not able to be subjected to accidents," he calls it "a predication according to the substance of the thing."

92. Having now shown the differences of nine predicates in their manner of predication, he at last turns to relation because the solution of the question depends on it.

V

1.   Thus he says: "Let us now speculate about the predicate of relation on account of which we have been outlining the other predicates for the sake of the argument. For these predicates, which are
clearly seen to perdure on account of something outside itself, especially do not seem to make a predication by themselves."

He now begins to examine and carefully consider the force of the
predicate of relation since this predicate, as if it were a principle
cause, compelled him to introduce those things which he has thus
far presented about the other predicates.

2.   This he clearly states: "Let us now speculate about the predicate
of relation on account of which we have been outlining the other
predicates for the sake of the argument," that is, what he has added
about the other predicates. Therefore since he has already shown
that, beyond the predicates of substance, quantity, and quality, the
other predicates predicate outside the thing, much more will it be
clear that a predication happens outside a thing in relation, which
always comes forth from somewhere else.

3.   A father is called a father according to an extrinsic cause, that is,
because he has a son. Therefore the predication of father and of any
other relation happens outside the thing. This he clearly demonstrates with the following example: a master is a master because of a
servant, a servant is a servant because of a master.

But this argument could seem weak because a white thing which
has whiteness in it but from which the whiteness is removed is no
longer thought to be white. The philosopher weakens the analogy
and its resultant objection by this argument, that the whiteness that
is a cause of a white thing belongs to that white thing. But servitude,
which is the cause of lordship, does not belong to a master. Rather a
certain power belongs to the master by which he rules a servant.
And because that power would be destroyed when no servant exists,
it is clear that that power belongs to the master not because of an
intrinsic cause, but through the master's extrinsic possession of a
servant.

4.   And so for this reason it is clear that relation in no way has the
power of altering a subject because it is not in the subject according

to itself, that is, "in that which is its being," but is compared with something else, that is, "with that which exists in another way." This truth becomes even more obvious when one considers that a relation does not always happen "to something else but sometimes to the same subject." For there can be no alteration or variety in an identity. This, however, can happen if a relation is made with some other thing, for then alteration and variety would follow.

5. This is therefore what the philosopher correctly teaches about relation from that point where he says: "Let us now consider relation" up to the place where he says: "For suppose someone is standing," etc. Here, because he sets forth the matter with such a lucid and clear style,[1] we can move along easily and simply, and since I am loath to make an easy thing more difficult, I shall hasten to give an explanation of his assertion that the predication of relation could not alter anything. He declares this when he says:

6. "For suppose someone is standing. If therefore I approach him on the right, he will be on the left compared to me. Not that he himself is left but that I approach on the right. Again I approach him on the left. In the same way he will be on the right. But being on the right is not said of his being, as white or tall is, but he happens to be on the right by my approaching him. And so that which is leftness or rightness is by and because of me, not at all because of him."

7. He sets forth an excellent and comprehensive example when he shows that one cannot understand a thing to be altered in any way in the predication of relation. And what he teaches in a specific relation he wishes to be recognized in all relations. Therefore if Plato approaches on the right side of Aristotle who is standing still, Aristotle will be on his left. Not that Aristotle, if no one were to approach on his right, "is left but" only because Plato or someone else approached him on his right. Likewise if Plato had approached Aristotle on the left, Aristotle, who was a bit earlier on Plato's left, is now truly said to be on his right.

8. However, Aristotle has not suffered anything whence he could truly be said to be changed either in or because of these alterations in the direction of approach. For since he perdures in substance, quantity, and qualities in which he was known before the approach of Plato, there is no reason why one can say that he has undergone any change. For what was said of him, first being left and a little later being right on account of Plato's approach, was not said of his being.

Wherefore the philosopher concludes universally that by the predication of relation there can be neither alteration nor change in a thing whereby it can be shown to be anything other than itself.

9. He continues along these lines: "Wherefore those things which do not make a predication according to the property of a thing in that which it is, cannot alter, change, or vary its essence in any way." The philosopher immediately introduces that which follows from his universal conclusion: "Wherefore if the father and the son are said to be in relation and differ in nothing other than relation, as has been said, then relation is not predicated to that about which it is predicated as if it were the thing itself and according to the being of the thing about which it is said. So it will not make an alteration in the thing about which it is said but there is an interpretation of the 'alteration' of the divine persons, even though this term is used in a way that is difficult to understand."

10. He asserts that every predication by which something cannot be shown to be a thing in no way alters or "varies the essence." However the predication of Father and Son does not show a thing to be something but rather to have something related to it. Therefore the predication of Father and Son cannot in any way show an alteration of the Deity but rather an alteration "of the persons" in the Deity because, "as has been said," the persons in no other way "differ than by relation alone."

11. But since "relation is not predicated to that about which it is predicated," that is, "since relation does not" show the thing to be what it is called, as if the relation itself was the thing about which it is predicated, and, moreover since the specific predication of relation happens not according to its essence but outside of it, hence it is clear that the substance of the Divinity cannot be varied in this way but only the persons themselves distinguished in the relations.

12. Careful attention must be paid here to the order as well as the meaning of these words. He says that the predication of relation "does not alter the Divinity about which it is predicated but if it can be called an alteration, it is more in the sense of an interpretation." This was confirmed by the exposition given by those individuals who were present at the Council which dealt with this question "which could scarcely be understood" before its confirmation by the Council.[2]

The question about this word "person" has been fought over at length. Some assert that the three *hypostases*[3] of the Greeks ought to be signified by this word, while others argue that neither the New nor the Old Testaments uses the word "person" of the Father or the Son or the Holy Spirit. The latter were finally compelled to confess that the Father and the Son and the Holy Spirit are persons because although neither the New nor the Old Testaments speak of "persons," neither do they contradict this use anywhere.

13. When Boethius says "which can scarcely be understood," he implies that since a person is an individual of a rational substance, he is thus wondering how three persons can be predicated of one substance and one substance of three persons. This wonder or hesitancy we discussed above satisfactorily.[4] He states that the predication of relation can never make an alteration in the Divinity by inserting something philosophers know *per se* that "there is truth to the axiom that in some incorporeal things distinctions (it must be added, about the Divinity) are made by differences, not spatially."[5]

14. For if "in some incorporeal things" other than the Divinity there are distinctions "by differences, not spatially," much more in the Divinity, where there are neither substantial nor accidental differences, can there be no spatial differences. And that there can be no spatial distinctions in the Deity he confirms by this reasoning, that God receives nothing extrinsically. So then the name of Father is received because "the begetting of the Son is substantial," namely coeternal, to the Father since he begets the Son from that by which he is Father, namely from eternity. This argument is far removed from natural things.

15. For there was man before there was a father or a son, because Adam was the son of no man and, before he was the father of sons, he was a man. Therefore from an extrinsic cause it happened to him that he was a father and was called a father. Since therefore the generation of the Son has been called substantial to the Father and since the name of Father can be seen to be predicated substantially of God, Boethius adds that the relation "Father" is a substantial predicate.

16. We can get this sense from these words of the author: "For it cannot be said that anything has been added to God so that he became Father. Nor did he begin to be the Father because the begetting of the Son is substantial to him, the predication of Father indeed being a relation." And immediately Boethius abbreviates the argument, as if it were an epilogue, which he set forth above in several places concerning the conjoined unity of the Father and the Son and the Holy Spirit according to essence, saying: "And if we remember all

the propositions made previously, so we may consider that God the Son proceeded from God the Father, and the Holy Spirit from both. Because they are incorporeal, they cannot be distinguished spatially" and so on up to where he says "therefore of the three. . . ."

17. It has now been proved that the Father and the Son and the Holy Spirit are not differentiated by anything except relation. This truth certainly becomes clear to us if we remember and understand the propositions for proving it which are located in the earlier parts of this work, that God the Son proceeds from God the Father, and God the Holy Spirit from God the Father and God the Son. "Because they are incorporeal," the three persons are distinguished "not at all spatially" since it is a most certain axiom that "in incorporeal things distinctions are made by differences, not spatially."

18. But because the threefold predication of the Deity as Father and Son and Holy Spirit can seem to argue for a plurality of gods, Boethius re-introduces a true objection which he made earlier against this error, namely, that there are no differences in God by which one person differs from another except that one is not the other. For, as has already been shown, they do not differ in genus or species or number. "And where there is no difference, there is no plurality at all; therefore there is only unity."

19. He again presents in summary fashion an argument which we have already explained with his other arguments: "Where differences are lacking, plurality is absent. Where plurality is absent, only unity is found." And finally he adds: "For nothing can be brought forth from God except God," as if to explain the matter with the clear assertion, namely, that God does not differ from God either substantially or accidentally. And therefore God the Son does not differ from God the Father, nor does God the Holy Spirit differ from God the Father and God the Son because nothing can be brought forth or proceed from God except God.

20. And although "God" is repeated three times, as was made clear in the aforesaid lucid explanation, "in numerable things a repetition of units does not make a plurality in every instance," that is, from necessity. And because the repetition of unity in God "does not make a plurality," it is safely concluded that the substance of the three persons is one when he adds: "Therefore the unity of the three persons has been suitably established."

VI

1. Boethius professes that this is a unity of substance, not of persons, when he adds: "But because no relation can be referred to its own self, inasmuch as that which is a predication according to itself lacks relation, the manifoldness of the Trinity is made in that there is a predication of relation, while the unity is preserved in that there is an indifference of substance and of operations and of any other predication which is said of the Trinity's essence."

2. He first makes clear that no relation can be predicated "according to itself" for every "predication which is according to itself lacks relation" because if no "predication which is made according to itself" is relation, no relation taken relative to itself can be predicated. And thus the triple predication of relation in God when one says God the Father, God the Son, God the Holy Spirit shows the number of persons since apart from relation there is no Trinity in the Deity.

3. He declares that through the indifference "of substance and operations and predication according to itself" there is only unity in God: "Therefore the substance maintains the unity; relation multiplies the Trinity." This section seems to contain a difficulty because, since he will soon say that the predication of relation is not always such that it is invariably predicated to differing things as a servant to a lord but sometimes to the same thing, this passage seems to be contrary to that place where he says that "no relation can be referred to itself."

4. But setting aside the multiple explanations of this passage, we have selected one which may remove this contradiction which we fear. This explanation will make it clearer and easier to understand in what follows that no relation can be referred to itself and that no relation taken relative to itself, that is, according to itself, can be predicated.

5. I define a relation taken relatively to be when the relation is predicated as an accident, as when someone is said to be the servant of someone else, as Davus is a servant of Symon.[1] But it is not taken relatively when the relation is signified by a substantive name, as when the servant of someone is said to be a servant, for here it is

predicated about the individual as though it were a species and according to itself.

6.   There follows: "And therefore only those things which are of relation may be applied singly and separately. For the Father is not the same as the Son nor are either the same as the Holy Spirit. Nevertheless the same God is Father, Son, and Holy Spirit, the same justice, goodness, greatness, and all things which can be predicated according to itself."

7.   After the philosopher says that a plurality of persons arose out of a single cause in the one substance of the Deity, he introduces as evidence for this truth that these three single relations distinguish those persons so that the name Son is not appropriate to the person of the Father just as the name Father is not appropriate to the person of the Son. Also the name of Father and the name of Son are not predicated of the Spirit of both just as the name of Spirit of both is not predicated of the Father or the Son.

8.   For "the Father is not the same as he who is the Son nor are either of them the same as he who is the Holy Spirit," although "nevertheless the same God is Father, Son, and Holy Spirit, the same justice, goodness, greatness, and all things which can be predicated according to itself." For whatever can be predicated according to itself about the Divinity preserves the unity of the divine essence and does not at all constitute a trinity. This must be carefully noted because this plural word *omnia* places a multiplicity in natural things, but in the Deity it signifies nothing other than simplicity.

9.   But now let us see what follows: "One must clearly understand that a relation is not always such a predication that it is invariably predicated toward something different, as a servant is to a master. For they are different. For every equality is equal to equality; like is like to like; the same is the same to that which is the same. And similarly the relation in the Trinity of Father to Son and of both to the Holy Spirit is of such a kind that one is the same to that which is the same."

10.   A great amazement can enter the minds of the hearers since it is often said that the Father and the Son and the Holy Spirit are one and the same, even though they are referred to one another by different relations. For this reason he introduces an analogy for something which no one can clearly or plainly express. This he does in the first place so that one may understand that "a relation is not

always such a predication that it is invariably predicated about something different," in name as well as in thing, "as a servant is to a master."

11. For here the things signified, namely servitude and lordship, are diverse. The names, however, servant and master, are different, just as those things are diverse about which servitude and lordship are predicated by these names, as Davus and Symon. But when we say: "Equals are equal to equal and like is like to like," although those things are diverse which are compared to one another by one name, nevertheless the relation is the same, that is, equality and likeness of comparison.

12. Also the names of those relations are the same: here "equal," there "like." And when we say "the same is the same to that which is the same," we express through this description of relation a comparison in a way more similar than the above mentioned ones to "the relation there is in the Trinity of the Father to the Son and of both to the Holy Spirit." The comparisons made by the first two relations to one another, that is, of equality and likeness, appear much less suitable to the relation that exists in the Trinity.

13. Boethius faults the first two relations because one cannot discover or find a clear analogy in the things of the world with all its defects for this special kind of relation: "It is a result of the transitory nature of the otherness found in natural things that this special kind of otherness cannot be found in any natural thing." And therefore when we think about the simplicity of the Divinity, we must not return to imaginings of natural things, but we ought to contemplate the invisible God in his simplicity by the intellect without any imagining, because, as he said earlier, "it is the duty of every educated man to try to form his faith according to reality."[2]

14. "But enough has been said about the proposed question. Now the subtlety of the question awaits the standard of your judgment. The authority of your decision will determine whether it has been set forth well or not."

The philosopher turns aside to the friends to whom he writes and he asks that they subtly adjudicate his solution for the question as far as it has been correctly argued by him and that by their authority they would examine the merits of the treatise. And after he has made this request of his friends, he says there must be rejoicing in the Lord should they find his argument for the solution meritorious because it could not have happened except by God's grace that so difficult a question about the Christian faith could be solved even though faith by itself, that is, of itself and without the introduction of arguments, may be most firm. Indeed, as the Apostle says, faith "is the argument of things unseen."[3]

15. This is what he says: "For if being helped by the grace of God we have presented a suitable set of arguments to support the proposition that is most firmly founded on faith by itself, then the joy of the completed work will return to him from whom the effect comes."

He delays no longer, but seeks forgiveness for himself should the question not be satisfactorily explained, for the good will of the powerless ought to be an excuse. And so he concludes with this little verse: "For if humanity is unable to ascend beyond itself, prayers will supplement whatever feebleness takes away." Thanks be to God!

The Gloss of
Master Clarembald
on
Boethius's Book

De Hebdomadibus

The Gloss

I

1. Some define that part of logic which is called "dialectics" by drawing its meaning not only from its genus but also from the matter on which it operates and from the instrument through which it operates on its matter. For they contend that dialectics is the science of discovering a general proposition from probabilities that either have or lack necessity. Indeed they hold the genus to be discursive science. They correctly designate its matter as a general proposition from which the dialectician, with his instrument, that is, induction or syllogism, draws a conclusion assembled from probabilities.

   Sophistics and demonstration, however, differ from dialectics in the quality of the instrument, as Aristotle attests. They are nevertheless occupied as dialectics is with a general proposition, that is, in the same matter, because "a sophistical syllogism either is from those things which seem to be probable but are not, or appears to be from probabilities which seem to be probable."[1] Whence since the first does draw a truth from false premises, it is a syllogism. But the second is not a syllogism, since it infers a falsity from probabilities or from things similar to probabilities.

2. Demonstration, however, is a science which syllogizes from that which is true and primary, or from such things which draw the necessity of their credence from the necessity of true and primary

things. Primary and true things are known *per se* and have no need of outside proof. Of such Aristotle says: "It is not necessary to seek the 'why' in scientific principles, for any one of them is its own credence."[2]

From such *per se* known and primary principles certain posterior ones can be known *per se* so that, since they draw the necessity of their credence from these, they have the powers of true and primary things and suffice by the working of their own offices. Whence Aristotle in the *Priora Analytica* proves the posterior modes through the four modes of the first figure, which are held to be known *per se,* and having proved them he introduces the proof of their necessity because the *per se* knowns proved are taken from the previous *per se* knowns.[3]

3. There are, however, two kinds of *per se* knowns: one general and common, the other belonging only to the most learned and requiring the capacity of near *intellectibilitas*.[4] The following can serve as examples of these two.

A solution to the question which we now seek to explain is limited by the *per se* knowns of the kind that asks something subtle of a weak mind. It is now time to set out what kind of question it is, so that the intention of the philosopher, having proposed it, is clear.[5] For he intends to solve the question of John the Deacon of the Roman Church, who, in a certain letter which is found today deposited in a number of church archives, urgently sought from Boethius a solution to the question.

4. For the solution to the question in this treatise promises to be useful in that from it the readers may learn that every goodness which they have has come from the First Good so that God may be glorified in all things by every creature and the goodness of the Creator be exalted above all with great praise and his wisdom be described as inexpressible.

The question itself is as follows: Are those things that exist good because they exist even though they are not substantial goods? He hides its solution with certain obscurity from the immature thinker lest, as Boethius himself confesses to fear, it be ridiculed and vilified after it has been laid open to fools. For as Saint Augustine wrote, "Good things in the Holy Scriptures exist in the depths of mysteries lest those mysteries be rashly vilified by a quick, vulgar intellect."[6]

Whence Macrobius justly reproves the curiosity of a certain philosopher Numenius who divulged the rites of the Sacred Eleusians with excessive vulgarity. Macrobius says the Eleusian goddesses appeared to Numenius in a vision with wounded mien and in whore's clothing, complaining that he had prostituted them as whores because he had completely exposed their holiness.[7]

5.   Boethius takes his method from the mathematicians, for he first sets out the *per se* knowns or common conceptions of the mind which he then leaves to our ingenuity to adapt in solving this question. We, with the divine grace arousing our confidence, are thus prompted to adapt each one of the *per se* knowns to the argument. And no one should presume to seek in treatises of this kind those three principle methods of teaching which Galen mentions at the beginning of his book entitled *Tegni*. "All teachings are of three kinds. They happen in this order. The first is from an understanding of the end that happens according to dissolution. The second is from the composition that happens because of the resolution of things discovered. The third is from the dissolution of the terms."[8]

Indeed these methods of teaching are only properly applied to the teaching of the arts. Therefore setting aside for now those axioms which must be set forth in order to deal with this question, let us hear how the philosopher addresses the friend to whom he writes.

II

6. "You ask that I clarify and explain a little more clearly from our heb-domads" that question "which contains the manner by which sub-stances that exist are good since they are not substantial goods. And this you say has to be done since" this "style of writing is not known to everyone."[9]

   We spoke a lot about the meaning of a "question" when we were ingeniously explaining the aforesaid question [on the Trinity]. There we supported our assertions about it as much by citation of authorities as by our own reasoning.[10] Wherefore we think those points ought to be reviewed, if anyone should feel the need, in that treatise.

   For the present let us consider that which we now pursue, namely the explanation of the proposed question. First, after he has invoked the grace of the Holy Spirit, we note those passages in the prologue where docility is prepared in the readers, where attention is stirred up, and where good will is grasped. Thus he stirs up our attention when he recalls "the obscurity of the question." He prepares docility when he promises to organize "a little more clearly the obscurity of the" proposed "question" asked by the deacon. He first elicits good will from the person to whom he writes when he says that he has enfolded the parts of the proposed question in a subtle investigation. He further elicits good will from the same person no less when he promises to accomplish those things that his friend has asked him to do.

   And so responding to the letter, which we have noted had been directed to him by John the Deacon, he immediately shows the knot of the question that John asked him to untangle and the arguments by which he can resolve it for him. Whence since this question is about those things which exist, whether they are good "because they exist," it seems fitting to explain what the philosopher means by the phrase "those things which exist."

7. Things are said to exist in three ways, namely in the Divine Mind, in matter, and in existing things.[11] Now they exist in the Divine Mind in such a way that *intellectibilitas* comprehends them. They exist in matter in such a way that they are signified by names. Also they exist

in existing things in such a way that whatever they are, we can know them by the senses.[12]

And indeed in the way that they exist in existing things, they are said to exist absolutely. But they exist according to something else in the Divine Mind and in matter. However from those things which have obtained their true actuality in existing things, certain notions are abstracted by the mind, but these are thought to be creatures by naive people. This is not at all true. For every creature subsists in actuality. Accidents, however, which are called notions, are united only in the receptacle of the mind.

Whence Priscian, when he assigns a twofold definition to voice, says: "The first definition is taken from substance; the other from a notion, that is, from an accident which the Greeks call *enoya*," that is, in the mind.[13]

Cicero also in his *Topica* says to Gaius Trebatius: "There are two primary kinds of definition: one of those things which exist, the other of those things which are understood. However I say things exist which can be discerned or heard or touched, as a farm, a house, a wall, and like things. Of those things which do not exist, I again say they do not exist which cannot be discerned or shown or touched, although they can be discerned by the mind and intellect, just as you define acquisition, guardianship and cognition by common usage."[14]

And so that the meaning of this truth may stand more firmly, the authority of St. Augustine, who does not know how to deceive any more than to be deceived, is introduced. He says: "Since of those things which exist, some are discerned by the senses and others by the mind, learned men preferred to separate them by proper names."[15] And that which is already known by the senses they want to call *ousia*; that however, which is thought by the working of the mind they wish to name *symbebicos,* that is, accident.

Pythagoras attributed true existence to those very things which Cicero denied to have existence but rather to be discerned by the mind. Priscian and Saint Augustine, however, although they did not openly deny their existence, asserted that they existed only as notions of the mind.[16]

Boethius repeats this view in the second prologue to his *Arithmetica,* saying: "We say things exist which neither arise in the intention nor are diminished by being removed nor changed by variations, but abide always in the proper power of their nature, being leaned upon by lesser things. These things are qualities, quantities, forms, magnitudes, smallnesses, equalities, habits, acts, dispositions, places, times, and whatever is found joined in some way to bodies. These indeed, as is shown by vigorous reasoning, are incorporeal and immutable substances in their own nature. But they can be changed through their participation in a body and move into genuine instability by the touch of something mutable. Therefore because these things, as has been said, have obtained their immutable substance and power from nature, they are truly and properly said to exist."[17]

And indeed we have diligently explained in the question about the unity of the divine substance and the Trinity of persons that those things are only declared to have true existence since, if they truly existed apart from matter in the way that we investigate them according to the mathematical method, they would have true existence because they would owe nothing to matter. Therefore it is clear that this question is concerned about those things which nature produces and which have received the name creatures, namely whether those same things "are good because they exist," since goodness is not in them substantially.

8.   In order to answer this question, let us proceed in this way. Because this question must be clarified by the hebdomads, we define *hebdomad* first as derived from a translation of the Greek word *ebdo,* which in Latin means "I conceive." Others claim it is compounded from *eb* which means "in" and *domas* which means "mind." And so the hebdomads are called common conceptions of the mind, for of all that is in the mind, they are most ready to assent to the truth, just as anything guided by its proper sciences is accommodated to the examination of doubtful things.[18]

For example: the positive rules of grammar are subservient to its faculty, common speech to orators, the highest propositions to dialecticians, and theorems of the square are proved by the elements. Therefore the teachers of these arts use a variety of these concepts.

9.   However the reason for the present question is that in substances there can be no substantial goodness. For good is not predicated of substances either as a genus or species or difference or definition. Whence if goodness is predicated substantially of any one substance, that thing would be good insofar as it is a substance; just as Socrates,

because he is a man, is an animal because he exists; and because he is a man, he is rational because he exists, and again he is a rational mortal animal because he exists.

For whatever is placed under anything in the order of predication because it exists receives that thing to which it is subject in the order of predication. And finally being itself cannot be predicated as a genus of substances because in comprehending the genus of a thing, even though not entirely, it can be understood what the thing is.[19] On the other hand, although a thing is said to exist, it is not necessarily understood what it is. Since, therefore, goodness is not the genus of being, nor is being the genus of goodness, nor is either the genus of natural things, it is not surprising that there is confusion especially if we take the words to mean "substances by virtue of that in which they exist are good."

10. For so some wish to gloss this passage.[20] But it is better that in this place we understand a substantial good to be such a good whose whole essence is goodness. This most certainly is good because it exists, that is, it is good because it exists. For this is a true conclusion: if God exists, he is good. But this is not the case with those things which flow from the First Good. For it is not because Socrates exists that he is a man, although it may be concluded by simple being that a man exists because Socrates exists.

But concerning the First Good, this always follows: if God exists, God is good. And it is the same by simple being, that if God exists, he is the Good. Since therefore none of the things which exist is a substantial good, that is, such that its very existence from beginning to end is goodness, it seems worthwhile to inquire in what way those things which exist may be good because they exist.

11. This is how this section ought to be glossed. For what was said in the preceding section is not useful here, because the word *quod* ought to be a conjunction, not a pronoun, in this statement: those things which exist are good "because [*quod*] they exist."

Therefore the deacon asks that Boethius solve this obscurity for him with those common conceptions of the mind suitable for the solution for the question, not taken from that kind of conception about common and general things, but from that kind of conception about natural things, that is, that kind which is not thought to be impervious to those educated in the innermost secrets of philosophy. And for that reason Boethius implies that in order to please

John he will provide a solution for this question from *per se* knowns of this kind, lest the question be laid open to vain and stupid men should it be proved from the common kind of *per se* knowns; that kind of proof can be clear to all. But it is not proper "to give holy things to the dogs" or "to cast pearls before swine."[21] Therefore he adds: "You say this must be done because the manner of this kind of writing is not known to all."

12. There are those who understand this passage in another way. John asks Boethius to elucidate the obscurity of the question for him from natural conceptions because few can learn or understand this way of writing, among whom he judges Boethius to be the most polished. Since indeed it could be conjectured that on account of the difficulty John may not have the perspicacity for this question, the philosopher presents to him the witness of an eager perspicacity: he embraced both parts of the contradiction with subtle investigation and ingeniously assigned reasons to support parts of it. This can be gathered reasonably from this line: "I am your witness to the eagerness with which you have already embraced the subject."[22]

13. There follows: "But I think over my *hebdomad* rather with myself and I keep my speculations in my own memory rather than share them with any of those wanton and frivolous persons who cannot be serious on account of [a] their jesting and laughing."

After he has shown that John the Deacon, who asked him for a solution of the question from the *hebdomad,* has embraced the various parts of the question with a thoughtful investigation, he acknowledges that there are such *hebdomad* found which ought to suffice for solving the questions. This he does for the sake of his own memory rather than laying his mind open to vain men who, some being wanton and others frivolous, can bear nothing without jest and laughing, that is, free and familiar. For the preposition *a* is found in many places possessing the force of the preposition *prae,* as in the Gospel where one reads, "And they were unable to haul the net on account of [a] the multitude of fish."[23] For pleasing themselves in their own discoveries, they reproach the discoveries of others through the imprudence of capriciousness.[24]

Or for other readers, *a* is taken as a preposition causally in this way: whatever is "joined together by" teaching, that is, brought together in its proper findings, the wanton call languid on account of the laughter and joking by which they are primarily motivated. And since the philosopher already has claimed to keep his own *heb-domad* in his memory and to conceal their meaning from pseudo-philosophers, he entreats the deacon to be satisfied, lest the obscurity attending on "brevity" offend him for Boethius could not allow the secret of the question to be made public to the vulgar. Rather for those who ascend to the highest level of wisdom by philosophy, he sets out the truth of the question which indeed must be regarded as a great occasion for philosophizing.

14. And indeed he reiterates this when he says: "Wherefore do not be opposed to the brevity's obscurities, which, since they are the faithful guardians of secret doctrines, have the while this advantage, that they speak to those who are worthy." But now let us hear what he adds: "Therefore I have set forth limits and axioms, as customarily happens in mathematics and other disciplines, by which I shall develop all that follows."

It is the custom of the mathematicians, when they intend to prove any problem, to introduce the scientific elements according to the proposed art from which they draw the conclusions necessary for the proposition. There is no doubt that this also "happens in other disciplines" because descriptions and axioms are set out in the *Praedicamenta* in order to show what follows of equivocals, univocals, and denominatives, and some other rules which in many ways are useful for the understanding of the predicates.[25] Also in the *Priora Analytica* the multiple obscurity of the tract which follows is elucidated by the given four modes of the first figure.[26]

III

15. Therefore from these things by which the question is delimited, the philosopher, borrowing a like example, gathers the natural axioms which, as we have promised, we will attempt to adapt to this argument. In this place it seems proper to note that, since "a common conception of the mind" is called "a statement which whoever hears it understands it," the word *enunciatio* has the power of the compound noun so that this "conception of the mind" is that "statement which whoever hears it understands it." Also the same speech by which a *conceptio* comes forth is reflected no less in the noun *enunciatio,* and thus *conceptio animi* and the phrase *enunciatio quam quisque probat auditam* are conjoined as one.

For it is the law of compound nouns that everything which the compound noun brings together receives the compound noun conjointly and single things receive it individually. Whence this difference is found between compound nouns and collective nouns, that those things which a collective noun embraces are subjected as a whole conjoined under a collective noun, but not at all as single things.

For example: all the men of Laon are one "people." However no one of the men of Laon receives the name of the collective whole. But in compound nouns it is otherwise for the individual part, such that, because the noun "man" is this part of speech noun and that noun "animal" is the same part of speech, all nouns are conjoined in this one part of speech.

In created things the same is found, so that, because any one simple and least part of fire is this element of fire, and likewise all the parts of fire, namely of this element, are this element of fire. For an element is the simple and least part of a composite body. Hippocrates called simple a thing which is alike in its parts since it exists in the same essence. However he understood a thing to be the same in essence which does not take composition from a genus subject to diverse accidents, so that the parts of this whole element of fire are entirely in a genus of the same qualities. And so in this consists the difference between simple and single things, that the single thing has parts which, as Aristotle says, are in principle *omogeneos;* but a simple thing lacks all division.[27]

And in the manner we mentioned above compounds differ from collectives. And according to my teachers the word *enunciatio* [statement] in this place must be read as a compound noun. However "a conception of the mind" can be called "a statement" and "a statement" can be called "a conception of the mind" without a compound meaning, because often we state what we conceive and we often conceive what we state.[28]

16. Let us now note how the philosopher sets forth the division of the conceptions of the mind. He says: "Of these there are two kinds. For one is common such that it belongs to all men, just as if you propose this: if you subtract equally from two equal things, what remains are equal, no one understanding it would deny it. But the other belongs to the learned only which comes from such common conceptions of the mind as this: whatever is incorporeal cannot exist in a place, and others which the learned grasp but not the vulgar."

He sets forth two kinds of *per se* knowns: one absolutely *per se* known, the other known according to something else. And he first presents an example of an absolute *per se* known: "If you subtract equally from two equal things, what remains are equal." The proof of this *per se* known can be found in continuous as well as discrete quantity. For let two equal spaces be set before us and let them be ten feet in length, keeping those spaces on their other sides equal in measured feet. Therefore having removed by subtraction two feet from both, "no one understanding" the *per se* known can deny that the spaces remaining are equal to one another because as much was cut off from one as from the other.

And in discrete quantity, that is, in number, the same thing occurs in calculations because if by the previous reasoning you have taken twos from two tens, what remains are equal to one another in being two eights.

17. Having so distinguished these, let us discuss according to the proposed lesson the example of the *per se* knowns which are received by the learned. For "those things which are incorporeal do not exist in a place." This *per se* known comes from a common *per se* known because it can doubtlessly be proved that nothing can exist without that which it requires as its property. It is the property of bodies to have three dimensions, namely such that it is long and wide and high. Therefore in length it is measured from front to back, in width

from right to left, and in height from top to bottom. And there is nothing in the universe of things which is able to receive these dimensions in itself except a body.

Since therefore only a body has each of these aforesaid dimensions, it is necessary that nothing incorporeal have in itself front or back, right or left, top or bottom. Therefore nothing incorporeal is in a place. For here "not to exist in a place" is understood to mean to lack every dimension. And neither is any continuous quantity a place except that it is occupied by a body.

Whence Augustine in his *Categoriae* says: "A place, since it surrounds a body, is occupied by the parts of that body, so it is divided by a common limit in whatever way the body is divided, and therefore it is necessarily called cohering, etc."[29] For it seems that there can in no way be a place if every body by which places are occupied reverts to nothing. Whence a world which no place circumscribes is "in no place." Rather it is the place of all creatures. However spirits indeed are not "in a place" because they lack the aforesaid dimensions although they can be moved locally. Whence in eternity just as there are no bodies so there are no spirits or anything other than that solitary and simple nature which exists as the underived and immobile spirit, unless someone wishing to be mad with Epicurus says that before time the void was filled with atoms.[30]

18. And in this way the first axiom can come from the aforesaid common *per se* known. Therefore he sets forth in this way the other proposed axioms whose meanings we will uncover and out of which certain things can be explained and understood more according to theology than according to another discipline.[31]

"Being is different from that which exists. For being itself does not yet exist. But what has received the form of being exists and consists."

He sets out the *per se* known for which he must provide proof and evidence since it is not absolutely *per se* known. He calls the First Good "being" because it is doubtlessly the "form of being." However he calls each subsisting thing "that which exists" because it participates in the primordial entity, that is, "the form of being." For every subsisting thing takes existence from that "form," as the Apostle testifies, because all things are from it and through it and in it.[32]

And so "being is different" from that "which exists" because "that which exists" participates in that primal form and exists through it.

But that form participates neither in itself nor in anything else, just as whiteness does not participate in whiteness. Whence whiteness is not a white thing.

Every participation is either in something prior or in something posterior. However it is impossible for God to participate in himself or in anything that is coequal with him because he is the first of all things. If, however, he does participate in something after him, it would be a necessity for that thing, not being a simple being. Truly therefore has it been said that "being is different from that which exists."

19. To prove this the philosopher adds briefly: "Being itself does not yet exist." As if he had openly said: "The form of being itself is not yet" an existing thing, that is, participating in an entity. Neither is it a subsisting thing because it is subject to nothing but is indeed a simple thing, as Saint Dionysius recalls in his *Celestis Hierarchia,* that it seems more to approach nothing than something.[33]

"But that which exists," that is, that which subsists, is a subsisting thing by participation in and by the work of that highest form. It must be noted that Boethius skillfully and carefully says: "it does not yet exist." In absolute necessity from eternity all things were made conjoined in a certain simplicity and in it all things are what they are, as John the first of the theologians testifies: "What was made had life in him."[34] And since "life in him" belongs to things descending through the necessity of conjunction to fate, already they clearly present themselves in definite possibility and subsist in fate.[35] Just so therefore the philosopher makes note of this descent from eternity, not saying it does not exist, but "it does not yet exist."

20. The third axiom follows: "What exists is able to participate in something. Existing itself participates in no way in something. For participation happens when something already exists. However something exists when it receives being."

Satisfied with the explanation of the second axiom he explains the third. For "that which exists," that is, subsists, "is able to participate in something," as a man, beyond that "which he is" substantially, "is able to participate" in quantities and in a diversity of many accidents. But "being itself," that is, the form of being, "participates in no way in something" because form exists apart from matter. Thus at first "participation happens when something already exists" composed of matter and form. When this may be "however," he adds saying: "when it receives being," that is, generation.

21.   The fourth axiom follows simply from those *per se* knowns preceding it because "that which exists," that is, subsisting in definite possibility, "is able to possess something beyond that which it itself is," that is, extrinsically. "But being itself," that is, the primeval entity, "possesses nothing admixed beyond itself" because it is what it is in itself and owes nothing to matter from which contagion all mutability comes forth.

    The fifth axiom is set forth disharmoniously as follows: "There is a difference between merely to be something and to be something in that it exists."[36]

    Remigius thought that "to be something" was the subject and "to be something in that it exists" was an accident of the subject.[37] It seems more proper to us to understand "to be something" as the accident of the subject and "to be something in that it exists" to constitute the subject of the accident. For a substance is said simply to exist. But an accident has a certain existence because of a substance. For above it was related how some philosophers attributed non-being to an accident.[38]

    Nevertheless since accidents are notions of the mind, we do not deny that an accident is something. But we do not concede that "to be something in that it exists" is a correct definition for accident in this passage because the words which properly explain this *per se* known are found in the next sentence. For the word "there" properly refers as an adverb to that which has the first place, that is, "merely to be something." However the word "here" is more properly applied as an adverb to that which is placed nearest, that is, "to be something in that it exists" when he says: "there an accident is signified, here a substance."

    All the more we are advised to choose this meaning according to the authority of Calcidius, who said it belongs to substance to exist simply and to exist in that it exists. Accidents, however, are merely things that do not exist absolutely but only through substances from which they are abstracted.[39]

22.   The sixth *per se* known to the learned follows thusly: "Everything that exists participates in that which is being so that it may exist. But it participates in another thing so that it may be something. And therefore that which exists participates in that which is being so that it may exist. But it exists so that it may participate in something else."

    One must explain this *per se* known thusly, that "that which exists" is understood to be something subsisting from matter and form. Whereas "being" is the form of being, as in the other *per se* knowns. From which "being" an entity, that is, something subsisting, takes its appellation in this way, as if a denominative. Therefore "everything that exists" before it can exist necessarily participates in the form of being merely "so that it may exist." It participates "in another thing," that is, in some later form, whether that be substantial or accidental, "so that it may be something," that is, either an animal or a rock or white or round or heavy or something similar to these.

And because it cannot be "something" unless it first exists from the form of being, "therefore" that entity really exists "which participates in that which is being so that it may exist. But it exists" first from the form of being "so that" then "it may participate in something else," that is, it receives a later form through which it is something, that is, this or that, or such and not so. Whence among the ten natural questions the first is that which asks whether the thing exists. When this truth is understood, one may then properly ask what it is and how big or of what kind and so forth, which are contained in the remaining predicates.

23.   According to some the seventh axiom follows; according to others it is not an axiom but proof of the preceding *per se* known. Whence it can be shown as if by opposition that "everything that exists participates in that which is being so that it may exist. But it participates in something else so that it may be something" because "everything simple," that is, what is form alone, "has as one its being and that which it is" because nothing else is predicated of it outside the subject when it is said "to exist" than when it is said to be something. As if it were said of God, "God exists" and "God is just." If, however, this is a seventh axiom, the same explanation for it must not be denied.

In the same way it can be properly said of the following *per se* known that either it is the eighth axiom or it is a proof of the previously explained *per se* known. For when he says: "In any composite thing, it is one thing to exist and another thing to be itself," the phrase "to be itself" is understood as that which subsists as composed from matter and form, the phrase "to exist" is understood either as that nature by which it exists or as the form of being from which it exists. This existence you find least of all in simplicity.[40]

24.   The ninth axiom concludes the list of the *per se* knowns. It is as follows: "Every diversity is discordant. But likeness must be desirable.

And what desires something else can be shown to be naturally the same as that which it desires."

Here he calls "diversity" the contrariness of dissimilitude so that because the dissimilitude of fire and earth are shown to have contrary properties throughout, as subtlety and sharpness and mobility in fire and as bluntness and corpulence and immobility in earth, they cannot be united except by the interaction of mediums.

Whence Martianus Felix Capella: "You bind the warring seeds of the world with secret bonds and encourage the union of opposites by your sacred embrace."[41] For dissimilar things naturally flee from one another just as similar things naturally attach to one another for that "which desires something" holds in itself naturally the very same quality as "that which it desires."

Reasons and causes are evident and clear in certain things. However the causes of others are entirely hidden to us in the hiding places of a recondite nature. For example: air divided through a medium easily flows back into itself, for in the separation of its parts it still holds the same qualities naturally in itself. The reason is the same in the separation of water for on account of a natural similitude the parts easily return to one another.

But fire in a different way flees any separation because it so preserves itself in its natural qualities that neither its parts nor its whole self is able to be changed into contrary qualities in any way whatever. This is less true of the other elements. For permanent things, insofar as they exist accidentally in natural things, can assume contrary qualities just as air, naturally warm and humid, can become cold and dry by accident.

This was proved in this way by philosophers in their ascent of Mount Olympus. For the coldness and dryness of the higher air prevented those who wanted to test whether there was any turbulent motion of air in the superluminaries from ascending onto Mount Olympus until the water was warmed by the fire's heat and humidified the air with steam. With this assistance they ascended up the side of the Mount. Those returning a year later with this same help found ashes in that same place lying entirely unmoved on a marble surface.[42]

In the violent cold the air froze and dried. However there is no doubt that water and earth can be reduced to contrary qualities in natural things through the heat of fire because water becomes warm accidentally and the power of fire seizes the very earth as nourishment for itself. And so in many situations similar to these the reasons are manifest. But other desirable knowledge is muted in the hiding places of nature in order to hide the causes of things from us. For we are unable to explain why adamant comes from iron and many other things.

25.   But now having explained the *hebdomad* let us see what follows: "Therefore these axioms which we have presented are sufficient. With the prudent interpretation of reason anyone can be readied for these arguments." He says that the *hebdomad* that he presented are sufficient for considering the question but, as we have stated above,[43] he commits to the prudent expositor of his treatise those which must be adapted to the individual arguments.

IV

26. "But this is the question. Those things which exist are good. For a common proposition of the learned is that everything that exists tends to the good. However everything tends to its like. Therefore those things tend to the good which are themselves good."

Before he explicates the obscurity of the aforesaid question, which is whether "those things which exist" can be "good" because they exist since they are not substantial goods, Boethius first proves that those things that exist are good. And indeed this is most proper and correct. For the question whether they are good because they exist would be foolish if he did not first establish that they are good.

Moreover he adapts for this proof two *per se* knowns of the learned, of which one is found only in his book *De consolatione philosophiae* in a clear assertion of the truth, which is: "everything that exists tends to the good."[44] The other is clearly part of the ninth axiom presented above, which is: "Likeness is desirable. And what desires something else can be shown to be naturally the same as that which it desires."

27. Therefore from these *per se* knowns the following argumentation is constructed: "everything that exists" tends "to the good." "Everything" which naturally tends to something else "tends to the similar. Therefore whatever things tend to the good are themselves good." The same thing can be confirmed from the first part of the ninth axiom: "Every diversity is discordant."

And so having declared that those things which exist are good, he forms into a question that very proposition which he already holds to be true and using a disjunctive syllogism he reduces both sides of the question to impropriety, as it seems, to anyone who wishes to argue against him. If those things which exist are good, they are good either accidentally or substantially. And this compels the person who strives to hold that they are accidentally good to this position, namely, that he denies an already accepted *per se* known, that is: "everything that exists tends to the good." Now the objector is compelled to hold the other side of the question, which is that those things that exist are substantially good, again, as it seems, he is driven to another impossibility, namely, that all things that exist are God.

Wherefore since to hold either part seems to result in impossibility, it remains that those things which exist cannot in any way be good, if the disjunctive itself is true. This Boethius summarizes as follows:

28. "But it must be asked how they are good: whether by participation or by substance." The opportunity presents itself here to recall that participation can be spoken of in many ways. For many collections of things held under the same genera or species or specified as subjects by common differences and accidents are said to participate in the names of what contain them.

Also things constituted under the predicates of the most general individual nature and of those things which are placed between it and the most general are not at all improperly said to participate in the differences themselves. Inferior things participate in higher for this reason that the genera of species do not complete the whole essence but rather they precede as parts. Likewise neither do differences.

Also individual things themselves participate in a way in the most specific because the most specific, although they bring about the whole substantial being in individuals, by no means perfect an individual status which necessarily comes from the collection of accidents.

In another way things are said to participate themselves in certain qualities and accidents. For accidents do not enter into subjects as parts. Nevertheless they are said to participate in them perhaps for the reason that universals are found distributed as accidents in many subjects, which, as they are considered in themselves, are rightly called parts of what contains them. The discipline of logic considers these aforesaid kinds of participation.

But the theologian, for whom participation must be explained according to the *intellectibilitas* in his field, many times explains participation as eminent, according to which Boethius says in another place: "God is one in nature. But nothing prevents many things from existing by the participation of the Divinity." Also in this work that very participation is noted where he says that everything "that exists participates in that which is being."[45] For being here means the form of being.

29. A caution must be introduced here because, since each part of the question has led to impropriety in correct reasoning, he has added a

certain sophistry where he infers that those things which exist are similar to the First Good. But why this is not so, the following will explain.

But in that reasoning which is if they are good "by participation, in no way are they good in themselves," we can perceive nothing fallacious. Indeed it is clear that the same thing happens in the participation of accidents. And he adds this example: "For what is white by participation is not white *per se*."

Proceeding from this point he introduces the opposite of what he explained, namely that those things which exist tend "in no way" to the First Good if they are good accidentally—for the discourse is about this. This can be rightly confirmed by that *per se* known: "every diversity," that is, contrariness of dissimilitude, "is discordant."

30. Nevertheless we do not agree that the second good tends to the First because it is similar to it. Why this is not so will be made clear later.[46] But because the second flows from the will of the First Good, it naturally strives to return to its principle. For just as the whole series of numbers beginning from unity is limited by unity, so every creature descending from the creating principle through a designated series strives to be returned to its one principle inasmuch as it serves its nature.

Also this similarity is found in human combinations. For whatever combinations exceed a combination of equity are called "natural distemperments" by the physicians. Whence, when they constitute four grades in the four primary qualities, they define a grade to be the discreet domain of a quality in a subject. Therefore natural distemperments seek similar, not contrary, things in food and drink. But accidentals seek contraries.

So Galen in his *Pantegni* while he is treating the signs of the stomach says: "Distemperments made from sicknesses differ from natural things in this for they seek contrary things, not similar things, and in this way are not natural things."[47] Therefore there is nothing strange if the second good, which flows from the good will of the First Good, strives to return to the sweetness of its own origin.

31. But let us study what follows next. Boethius says, "But it has been agreed." It does not follow from this agreement that those things which exist because they are good accidentally tend to the good. It remains that its contradictory is false because earlier he made clear

by a common conception of the mind that what was introduced was true. Whence what follows it is false. And for that reason the philosopher removes it when he adds this: "Therefore they are not good by participation but by substance."

Here you must guard against a fallacy when he argues that those things which exist are substantially good. For it is necessary for you to remember the three participations of things recalled above, except the one which they have in names.[48] However one must read this with the sense that that twofold division seems sufficient and that those things which exist are good substantially, that is, in that they exist, just as the First Good is good in that it exists. For if this is so, the goodness of those things which exist is a subsisting thing.

If, however, the goodness of those things which exist is a subsisting thing, "that which they are," that is, "what they are" would be goodness. The philosopher holds this view strongly: "Of those things whose substance is good, that which they are are good things."

32. There follows: "However that which they are they have from that which is being." This verse can be explained theologically. And it can also be seen as inserted here according to logic. For "that which" things "are they have from that which is being," that is, from the form of being from which they come forth according to one part of the sixth *per se* known: "Everything that exists participates in that which is being so that it may exist." One can likewise explain according to logic how inferior things are said to take substantial being from higher things. For thus does man, in that he exists, have his being from humanity, which is his being, just as the nearest genus constitutes something with its own differences.

If, therefore, goodness is a substance for those things which exist and "that which they are they have from that which is" its "being," it is clear that "the being of all things is good," that is, goodness. "But if the being of all things is" goodness, the things themselves are good things "in that they exist" and "it is the same in them to be and to be good," just as of men "it is the same to be and to be" a rational, mortal animal.

This, therefore, is what the philosopher says: "Of those things whose substance is good, that which they are are good things. However, that which they are they have from that which is being. Therefore their being is good. Therefore the being itself of all things is good. But if being is good, those things which exist in that they exist are good things. And it is the same for them to be and to be in good things," that is "as to be" good things.

But according to the agreement of the adversary, he properly infers that the being and the goodness of things is the same when he adds: "Therefore they are substantial goods because they do not participate in goodness," that is, goodness is substantial for them. Or rather "they are substantial goods," that is, from their being "they are good things because" it appears that they are not good things accidentally since for them it is the same to be and to be good things. Indeed if they were good things accidentally, it would not be "the same for them to be and to be good things" just as for a raven it is not "the same to be and to be" black.

33. There follows: "For if for them their being is good, there is no doubt but that, since they are substantial goods, they are like the First Good. And through this they will be that Good itself. For there is nothing like to it except itself. Therefore it happens that all things that exist are God. But it is impious to say this."

Above the philosopher admonished the reader that he must ask in what way those things which exist are good, whether accidentally or substantially. After he has argued that they are good substantially, he reduces this position to impropriety by skillful argumentation because if "the being" of things "is" goodness, as the divine essence is, it is clear that all things which exist are "similar to the First Good and" moreover they are "that very" First "Good itself" to which "nothing" can be "like except itself." Whence you must carefully attend to what he says: "For there is nothing like to it," to the Highest Good, "except itself."

For just as unity is said to be equal to itself and the same to the same, so it is asserted here that that First Good is like to itself.[49] If, therefore, those things which exist are like the First Good in the property of his essence, since there is "nothing like to it except itself," without doubt it is true that "all things which exist" are that very First Good. That very First Good, however, is God. Therefore "all things which exist" are "God. But it is impious to say this."

To confirm this Boethius adapts the seventh axiom: "Every simple being has as one its being and that which it is." God, however, is simple form and outside matter. Wherefore "it is impious to say" that those things which exist are God" for according to the eighth axiom "in every composite being, it is one thing to exist, it is another to be something."

34. Let us see what follows next: "Therefore they are not substantial goods. And so for them being is not good." So it is that the desire to hold that those things which exist are substantially good things leads one to the most absurd impropriety. There is, however, a *per se* known for this: that which follows an impropriety is likewise improper.[50] Therefore he removes the impossible absurdity when he says according to logic that those things which exist "are not therefore substantial goods for this reason," that is, from this connection of consequences, "being in them is not good," as if he had said that the goodness of those things which exist is not a substance.

After introducing that which seems to follow from this line of reasoning he concludes briefly, "Therefore they are not good things in that they exist." Next he removes the other part of the division which the adversary held when he repeats the impropriety which follows from it. He concludes from this part, although by a fallacy, that those things which exist in no way are good things. He says, "But neither do they participate in goodness. For in no way do they tend to the good. Therefore in no way are they good things."

Therefore having introduced contrary views to the question, Boethius produces the solution by careful reasonings. As often happens in very difficult arguments, he makes use of an impossible position with the consent of his adversary. This is what the Greek philosophers call *hypothesis*. For by doing so, he sets up two goods, namely the first and the second. Of these the essence of the first is nothing other than goodness. And that goodness is nothing other than its essence. It is impossible for anything to come forth from this good unless it is a good thing.

The essence of the second good is not goodness because it comes from the First Good. However neither is it accidentally nor substantially good. Rather it exists out of a creating principle from which it is impossible for something other than the good to come forth. Above we made mention of this participation.[51] Indeed every being participates in the goodness of its creating principle. And, therefore, from this impossible position and from a recognition of the two types of good, the solution to the question is found. And it is clear why the second good is not like the first.

V

35. Therefore he says: "This sort of solution for the question can be allowed. There are many things which, although they cannot be separated in actuality, may nevertheless be separated in the mind and in thought. For example, although a triangle or anything subject to matter cannot actually be separate, however in the mind we can speculate by separating the triangle and its properties from matter."

Although it seems abhorrent to hold by the power of human reason through an hypothesis that the Divine Presence, which is everywhere whole, does not exist, we are encouraged to proceed in this way based on the example of the mathematicians. Boethius instructs those who follow the scientific method to abstract in the intellect and judge by the mind those things which exist actually and truly in material subjects and which cannot be separated from it naturally.

For example: A triangle or a sphere cannot be separated from material subjects in true actuality. However "in the mind" a mathematician can speculate about triangle and sphere and any other subjects outside the matter of their true existence. Whence he judges and defines those things as if they were outside of matter. Here let us present an example. Boethius calls "the sphere a roundness having the same semicircular diameter."[52] For it is a property of these things, which the mathematician investigates in their truth, to be considered outside of matter. However we said many things along these lines in the question of the Holy Trinity.[53]

36. But now let us return to the proposition itself. Boethius says: "Therefore let us remove from the mind for now the presence of the First Good, upon whose existence there is indeed agreement. For that presence can be known from the propositions of all the learned and the unlearned and even from the religions of barbarian peoples."

In seeking a solution to this question, the philosopher begs to remove from the mind "the presence of the First Good," that is, the First Good which is present everywhere. And indeed "for now," that is, for a while, until a solution of the question is found by this removal. "Indeed which" good, although it is held not to exist as an example in order to solve the question, nevertheless it is understood "to exist" most truly because the universe of creatures agrees that it exists. For there is no rational creature who does not venerate something as divine.

"Having removed this good for now," as has been explained, the philosopher makes use of another position: given the possibility of the existence of the First Good, it is impossible to remove it for "all things that exist are good things." Therefore having now set down two positions, one simply impossible, the other hypothetically possible and impossible, he calls upon us to consider how "those things" which exist "can be good things if they have not descended from the First Good." The following passage bears this meaning: "Therefore having removed this for now, we hold that all things that exist are good things. And we consider how they can be good if they do not flow out from the First Good."

37. There follows: "From this I consider it one thing in those things that they are good and another that they exist." After he teaches us to remove from our mind for now the presence of the First Good as an example for solving the question, he finally clarifies how that affects the solution of the question. For since now there is not a First Good, but there is a second and it is good, it cleverly appears in our considerations that "in those things" which "exist" it is "one thing that they are good," that is, for one reason to be good things, and "another that they exist," that is, for another reason to subsist.

But since the First Good does exist, as indeed he most truly exists, those things which exist without doubt have existence and are good from the same good, that is, from himself. Therefore with the agreement that the First Good does not exist, those things which exist are good from accidental goodness, but they exist from their own substances. Therefore for one reason they exist and for another they are good.

In order to prove this truth he introduces a fitting example: "One and the same thing is held to be good, heavy, round, white." For if this is held, it appears evident that for one reason the thing "is that substance"—certainly from its own substantiality—and for another reason it is called and it is "round," indeed from rotundity, and for another reason it is called and it is "heavy from heaviness," for another reason "white," without doubt from color, for another reason "good," without doubt from goodness. For this is what he says: "Then it is for one reason that substance belongs to it, for another rotundity, for another color, for another goodness."

The truth of this is made clear from the fifth axiom: "There is a difference between being something and being something in that it exists; the former signifies an accident, the latter a substance." And since he has distinguished "singular things" in this way, because it can be seen by anyone that all these are one because they make one actual thing, he introduces an *antipophora,* that is, a reply to a tacit objection, saying: "For if these individual things were the same as its substance, heaviness would be the same as color," as rotundity, and "as good; good would be the same as heaviness." And so opposites become one "simple thing" in identity, for it would have as one "its being and that which it is." But "nature," i.e., the diversity of predicates, does not allow this to happen.

38. But because "nature does not allow" this, for in natural things it is "one thing to exist and another to be something," that is, to be long or short or good or round or heavy. This is what he says: "Therefore it is one thing for them to be, another to be something" because they participate singularly "in being" so that they may exist, but they participate "in something else," that is, in the good accidentally, "so that they may be something."

And so, if it is agreeable to take *esse* [being] here in a logical sense, the sixth or the eighth of the *per se* knowns can be accommodated. For the sixth is as follows: "Everything that exists participates in that which is being so that it may exist. But it participates in another thing so that it may be something." The eighth is: "In any composite thing, it is one thing to be and another to be itself."

"And thus," according to this position, "they may be good things." But "nevertheless their being" is not "good" because they have goodness only by accident, as a white man has whiteness. For although a man is white, he does not have a white being.

Likewise one can adapt here the third *per se* known, if it is agreeable to interpret *esse* logically, which is as follows: "What exists is able to participate in something. Being itself participates in no way in something." For accidents are not contained in genera and species and differences, in which the being of things consists.

Well, let us proceed: "And thus they would be good. However not at all would their being be good." In the reality of existing things, although goodness is not in them substantially, "nevertheless" they have their "being good" from their operative form. Nor ought anyone suggest that goodness is either substantial or accidental in the creature because this is a judgment of theological reasoning which exceeds all rules of logic. For it is only proper to explain this according to *intellectibilitas,* as we discussed elsewhere.[54]

39. Now let us hear what he infers from what he has just said. "Therefore if they exist in any way, they would not be good or from the good. Nor would they be the same as the good. But for them existence would be one thing and being good another."

If we hold these positions, those things which exist would be good. "However not at all would their being be good." Whence it is not unreasonable to infer that if those things have not received their goodness from the First Good, then "they would not be the same as the Good." But according to the second *per se* known, "Being is different from that which exists," "to exist is one thing for them, and to be good is another."

Now the opposite case. They are "the same as the Good" as a man is the same as animal. For if they have not come forth from the First Good, but are accidentally good, "they would not be the same as the good," just as Rutenus is not the same as white.[55] For although every Rutenus were white, it would not follow that if Rutenus exists, he is white. For what is not necessarily true now may be true at some later time. Indeed Rutenus is white only contingently. However it must be noted that in this conjunction, which unites the consequent to the antecedent, *tunc* [then] must be read as an adverb, just as by common usage we are accustomed to say "if this exists, then that exists."

40. There follows: "For if they were nothing at all except good and there was in them neither weight nor color nor spatial dimension nor any quality, they would be nothing other than good. Then they would not appear to be things, but the principle of things," because all would be one, according to the seventh *per se* known which is: "Everything simple has as one its being and that which it is."

Whence he briefly adds: "Not they would seem, but rather it would seem." And thus the philosopher seems to correct his statement because he spoke plurally of a simplicity: "they would seem." Wherefore again he adds: "For it is one and the same kind of thing which is only good and nothing else," just as it is found in the fourth *per se* known: "Being itself possesses nothing admixed beyond itself."

But those things which exist are not at all simple things because, as is found in part of this same *per se* known, "that which exists can have something other than what it itself is," as a man, beyond that which he is as a rational mortal animal, "can have" height, width, weight, color, and other similar things, and numerous changes in these.

But man is not these things. Rather he has received at one time those things which constitute him. Therefore since those things which exist "are not simple things nor can they exist" in any way "except" through the form of being, "for the reason" that, because they have being through that which is nothing other than goodness, they themselves are good things. For just as a white thing is what whiteness informs, so it is necessary that there be a good which furnishes the good substantially.

As that which exists according to reason exists through rationality, so that which exists through the primal goodness is necessarily a good being. Indeed just as qualities in natural things give accidental denomination to their subjects, so does supersubstantial goodness impress goodness on its creatures, as theological reasoning determines it to be as if a mean between substantiality and accidentality.

And you can gather this meaning from these statements: "Because those things are not simple things, neither could they exist at all unless that which is the only good willed them to exist. For this reason, because the being of them flows out from" goodness, "they are said to be good." And to prove this truth, he distinguishes the First Good from the second, showing that because the essence of the First Good is goodness, both his goodness is the same as his essence and nothing else can be predicated of him through his being as through his goodness. Thus "because he exists, he is good."

41.   But although the goodness of the second good is not its essence, nevertheless it is necessary that its being be good because nothing that is not good can descend from that goodness that is supersubstantial. This he holds emphatically: "For the First Good is good because it exists. But the second good is good because its very being flows from the First and so it is also good." And then so that the evidence may be clearer, he adds this to the argument: "But the very being of all things," which has been shown undoubtedly to be good, "flows from that which is the First Good and which is so good that rightly," that is, properly and truly in itself, "is it said that it is good because it exists."

But because that First Good is properly and truly and in itself good "because it exists, the second good," which participates in that first principle of goodness, having taken its existence from it, "also is good" since it exists "because" it does not receive accidental goodness in itself from the primal goodness. And so he continues in this way: "Therefore their being is good. For then it is in the First Good."

42.   There follows: "In this way the question is solved." The question is doubtlessly solved in this way especially because good has been shown to exist in two ways. One is the First Good whose essence is goodness. The "second" could not exist unless it were good because the second, which by a certain denomination can be called "good," comes forth from the first, for it could not exist unless it were good. Whence it is concluded that it is "good because it exists" although, however, not in the same way by which the First is good. Likewise that which is done justly by a just man becomes just precisely because of the just man and is rightly called "just" by common usage.

And since the first as well as the second is called "good because it exists," the second is not for that reason the same as the First for the First is good in every way and substantially and for this reason "because it exists." But the existence of the second good is only good because it comes forth from the First. Nor can it be good in any other way "because it exists."

Therefore it is not the same as that from which it exists, because that is Good absolutely "because it exists" and is not indeed anything but good. However that thing, if it did not exist from it, could be taken to be good at least accidentally through an hypothesis. However simply because it exists, it can be taken to be good because then it participates in the adjective goodness. But since it would not have its being from the First Good, its being could not hold its goodness, just as a rock whose being is white accidentally, because it is made from genus and difference, does not itself have white although existing as white. And in this way a confirmation of the solution to the proposed question can be taken from the words which are in the following passage:

"For this reason, although they are good because they exist, they are not, however, similar to the First Good because in whatever way things exist, their existence is not their good. But because the being of things cannot exist unless it flows from the First Being, that is, the First Good, for that reason that being is good. But it is not like to that one from which it exists. For that thing, in whatever way it exists, is good because it exists. For it is nothing other than good. This, however, does not exist except from the First Good, though perhaps it could be good, but it could not be good because it exists, for then it could perhaps participate in the good. But its being, which it does not have from the good, could not hold the good."

Therefore let the reader note, if there perchance will be any, how the single elements of this passage set in orderly fashion up to this point explain those things which we introduced as a solution of the question, except that we made mention of the twofold good early in the discussion in order to confirm the matter.

43. Finally let us proceed: "Therefore having removed the First Good from these things in mind and understanding, although these things are good, nevertheless they could not be good because they exist. And because they could not in actuality exist except that which is truly Good produces them, for that reason their existence both is good and is not like the substantial good from which they come. And except they come forth from it, although they may be good, they could not be good because they exist and they would be other than the good and not from the good, since that alone is good who is the First Good and Being itself and Good itself."

Earlier when he attempted a solution in order to explain this matter, he used two hypotheses, one impossible, the other possible. From these the whole force of the solution emanates. Now as if in an epilogue he repeats each hypothesis with a summary of the previous arguments so that, having recalled the arguments with each of the hypotheses, he can keep the solution to the question most firmly in his memory.

And where he says: "Having removed the First Good from these things in mind and understanding," he repeats the impossible position of those things which have been created. But where he adds: "Although those things may be good," he repeats the possible position. However, when he says "nevertheless they could not be good because they exist," he implies the accidental goodness things would have if, being removed from the First Good, they were good things.

So he holds that a thing could not "exist except that that which is the true good produces it" and "for that reason its being would be good." He reproduces here the argument with which he proved that the existence of things is good because they exist, but not for the reason that the second good is like the First. He expands on this adding: "And except they flow out from it although they may be good," as if he were to say: not from the Good, "nevertheless they cannot be good because they exist because they would be apart from the good," that is, entirely removed from the Good, and "not from the Good since" in the truth of simple essence "that is good who is the First Good and being itself," that is, that eternity by which time and all temporal things descend. Just as he says elsewhere:

> You who order time to go forth from eternity and,
> remaining stable, give movement to all things.[56]

And since that itself is the First Good of all good things and eternity itself, it is also "being itself," that is, simple, "and the good itself," that is, such that it does not exist except that it is good and that it does not exist except that its existence is good because according to the seventh axiom "its being and that which it is are one."

VI

44.   Well, let us run over briefly what follows since we have covered the more difficult material. He says: "But will it also not be necessary that white things be white things because they exist as white things since they flow from the will of God so that they be white? Not at all. For it is one thing to be something and another thing to be white. This is because he who makes things that they may exist is indeed good, but he is not at all white. Therefore it is attendant upon the will of the Good that they are good things because they exist. But a property of such a kind is not attendant upon the will of what is non-white, such that it is white because it exists. For they do not flow from the will of something white. But because he, who is non-white, wills them to be white, they are merely white. But because he, who is good, wills them to be good, they are good because they exist."

He seems to raise this objection on account of a similarity to the same type of causality because, since those things which are good because they exist are good, in that they flow from the will of the First Good, white things seem to be white because they exist because white things emanate from that same will. But he says that this is "not at all" true because in those things which are good, it is the same to be and to be good. But in white things it is not the same to be and to be white. This is the case because "he who makes" single things "that they may be" good "is good" substantially. However he is not "white." For if he himself were substantially white, then those things created from him would be white because they exist.

And because he who wills that those things exist is nothing other than "good," they are good because they exist. But because he is not white "who wills that they be white, they are merely white," that is, not because they exist. "But they are good because they exist because he who wills them to exist" is nothing if not "good," as has been said.

45.   There follows: "According to this reasoning, therefore, is it necessary that all things be just because he who wills them to exist is just? No indeed. For being good refers to essence, but being just to

action. However it is the same in him to exist and to act. Therefore it is the same to be good and to be just. But it is not the same for us to be and to be just. For we are not simple beings. Therefore it is not the same for us to be good and to be just. But existence is the same for all of us because we exist. Therefore we are all good, but we are not all just. Further: good is something general, but just is specific. A species does not come down into all. For this reason some are just, others something else, but all are good."

He puts forth an objection which can be made about similar things on account of the same causality. Certainly by the former reasoning it was necessary that those things which are white are not white because they exist because he who made them to be white is not white. But he who made them to be good because they exist is good. Whence because he who made all things is just, all things would appear to be just by the same reasoning.

But the philosopher does not agree to this for this reason, that in creatures it is the same to exist as to be good because the being of any creature is good. But the being of any creature is not just. For although in God it is the same to be just as to be good, kind, pious, and other like things, however in creatures to be just refers not to substance but to activity. For justice is a constant and perpetual will for the distribution of equity. However, distribution is an action, not an essence. Therefore it seems to have been well said that justice in us "refers" not to essence but "to action." But in God it is not so because in him "it is the same to exist and to act."

46.   But a bit of a question occurs to us as we have discussed the question above. God exists and did not begin to exist. However it appears that at sometime he did begin to act. Moses wrote: "In the beginning God created heaven and earth."[57] Also in many other passages of the Divine Scriptures it may be read that God made this and that. Therefore how can we say that in God "it is the same to exist as to act?" For his existence is without doubt eternal. But to act seems to be temporal. Now we could say that although he who is eternity never began to exist but at sometime began to act because although the prudence of acting never receives a beginning in him, "it is the same in him to exist and to act."

Or we can treat this question in another way. Indeed to act in God is to speak, as the Psalmist says: "He spoke and they were made. He ordered and they were created."[58] His speaking is his willing. However his willing is his kindness. But his kindness is his essence. Therefore it can truly be said that in God "it is the same to exist and to act." For his existence is the same as his goodness. "Therefore it is the same in him to be good as to be just." However it is not so "for us," as the philosopher says, because "we are not simple beings" as God is. This can be confirmed from the fourth *per se* known: "That which exists is able to possess something beyond that which it itself is. But being itself possesses nothing admixed beyond itself." And the same confirmation comes from the eighth axiom: "In every composite thing, it is one thing to exist and another to be something."

Therefore because it has not falsely been said that good refers to essence and just to action, although he is just who makes us that we may exist, we, however, are not just because we exist because justice does not come down to us from the will of acting with equity. But our goodness is from the goodness of the Creator himself. Whence "in all of us existence is the same because we exist," that is, we are good but not just.

And moreover there is another solution for this objection, namely that "the good is general, but just" is a species of the good. The general good flowing from the Creator embraces all things in a creature, if indeed, as Plato noted when writing about the constitution of the sensible world, "the world has been made similar to nothing specific, because perfection lies in the genus not the species."[59] It is clear that Plato certainly attributed that type of perfection to the world. And since just, as had been said, is a species of the good, but every species is part of its genus, "a species" cannot come down "into all." And for this reason through division it is found to inhere in some things. The philosopher implies this division when he brings his work to an end: "Therefore some things are just, others something else, but all are good."

47. Now that we have surmounted the difficulty of the question and adapted the common conceptions of the mind in their proper places according to our purposes, we have nonetheless overlooked a certain matter that we think should be treated at this time. We have delayed its consideration until the end so that one may understand it more clearly after disentangling this intricate work. For it would not have been wise for us to say earlier all that could have been said about the question because its difficulty pressed upon us more strongly at that time.

The good was spoken of in different ways: in one way as that which is in every way and absolutely good and as something else which takes its goodness from that First Good. Since we have used the word 'good' differently in our discussion, we shall now define the second "good" as something "ordered" which truly flows from the First. But that from which the second good flows is rightly understood as ordering all things. For just as Moses said: "God saw all that he had made and they were very good."[60] God calls them very good because they are ordered in the very best way so that as a result nothing in the kingdom of Divine Providence can be considered accidental. Whence it is even written that the Divinity created, that is, ordered evil.[61]

Plato agrees with this truth: "Nothing happens whose origin lacks legitimate cause and reason."[62] Boethius also in *De consolatione philosophiae* does not deny that Divine Providence governs all things wisely so that God even changes to good the evil which we do.[63] As indeed, by the divinely ordered reason, good follows from evil just as in a similar way the true follows from the false. Therefore all things are ordered to the good which flow from the ordering principle. For it would not be called a principle ordering all things rightly if the things descending from that principle could not be called ordered.

And in this way it has seemed to me and to my teachers that the good ought to be understood here.[64] However, if it seems to be otherwise to someone else, if nonetheless the good is well defined, we shall not calumniate the good.

Notes

Notes to Translators' Introduction

1. Wilhelm Jansen, *Der Kommenter des Clarenbaldus von Arras zu Boethius De Trinitate,* Breslauer Studien zur historischen Theologie 8 (Breslau: Müller & Seiffert, 1926), 148.

2. Nikolaus M. Häring, *Life and Works of Clarembald of Arras,* Studies and Texts 10 (Toronto: Pontifical Institute of Medieval Studies, 1965). All references to the texts of Clarembald will follow the numbering and pagination in the Häring edition: each entry will indicate the gloss, the book and section number, and the page number. The gloss on the *De Trinitate* will be abbreviated as *DTr* and that on the *De Hebdomadibus* as *DHeb.*

For a more recent study of Clarembald's glosses, see John R. Fortin, *Clarembald of Arras as a Boethian Commentator* (Kirksville, Mo.: Thomas Jefferson University Press, 1995).

3. *Gallia Christiana* 3.35 (Paris: Victor Palmé, 1870–). It might be noted here that the various spellings of Clarembald's name occur in this entry: "Clarembaldus *al.* Clarenbaldus et Clarebaldus." The first spelling is adopted here.

4. *DTr, Epistola* 1:"Cum regimini scolarum accitus ab episcopo Laudunensi, qui nunc Urbi praesidet . . . " (Häring, 63).

5. *E vita et miraculis S. Thomae a Willelmo monacho Canturarensi editis* 2.89 in *MGH SS* 27, 37 (11–13).

6. *Gallia Christiana* 3.327D. Enzo Maccagnolo speculates that Clarembald's third known work, a treatise on the six days of creation, *Tractatulus,* was offered to Queen Matilde, the mother of Henry II of England, in an effort to elicit her support on behalf of Becket during his exile. See "La destinataria della 'Epistola' di Clarembaldo di Arras," *Scandalion* 3 (1980): 315–18.

7. *DTr, Epistola* 3: "non quo mei viribus ingenii confiderem sed ut doctorum THEODORICI BRITONIS et HUGONIS DE SANCTO VICTORE, apud quos in hoc opere vehementem operam dedi, lectiones imitarer" (Häring, 64).

8. The manuscripts of this massive text (MSS Chartres, Bibliothèque mun. 497–498) were destroyed by fire in 1944 during World War II, but microfilms of them

survive. The *Prologus* has been edited by É. Jeauneau in *"Le Prologus in Epta-theuchon* de Thierry de Chartres," *Medieval Studies* 16 (1954): 171–75. G. R. Evans lists and identifies the contents of the text in "The Uncompleted *Heptateuch* of Thierry of Chartres," *History of Universities* 3, ed. Charles Schmitt (Amersham, England: Averbury, 1983), 1–13.

9. This text has been edited by Charles H. Buttimer in the Catholic University of America Studies in Medieval and Renaissance Latin 10 (Washington, D.C.: Catholic University Press, 1939).

10. See n. 4 above.

11. See for example the comments in II.7: "Et nos quidem haec supra quaestionem de unitate divinae substantiae et personarum Trinitate diligenter explicavimus" (Häring, 193) and in V.35: "De huiusmodi autem in quaestione de sancta Trinitate plura diximus" (Häring, 211). This gloss also has a less formal ring to it: there is little manifest reliance on Thierry, who is not even mentioned; Clarembald appears at times to be citing Boethius from memory; there is more frequent use of interlinear comments than in the *DTr* gloss. Perhaps Clarembald was more comfortable with this text and considered it less formidable than the former.

12. See n. 6 above.

13. The references to the theological treatises of Boethius, unless cited by Clarembald in his glosses, are taken from the edition of H. F. Stewart, E. K. Rand, and S. J. Tester in *The Consolation of Philosophy and the Theological Tractates*, Loeb Classical Library 74 (Cambridge, Mass.: Harvard University Press, 1973).

14. For an interesting discussion of this method, see Mechtid Dreyer, "Die literarishe Gattung der Theoremata als Residuum einer Wissenschaft *more geometrico*," in *Philosophy and Learning: Universities in the Middle Ages*, ed. M. J. F. M. Hoenen, J. H. Josef Schneider, and Georg Wieland (Leiden: E. J. Brill, 1995), 123–35.

15. For the writings by Thierry or attributed to Thierry in the *opuscula*, see the collection edited by N. M. Häring in *Commentaries on Boethius by Thierry of Chartres and His School*, Studies and Texts 20 (Toronto: Pontifical Institute of Medieval Studies, 1971). The glosses of Gilbert, likewise edited by Häring, are found in *The Commentaries on Boethius by Gilbert of Poitiers*, Studies and Texts 13 (Toronto: Pontifical Institute of Medieval Studies, 1966).

16. For Gottschalk, see *Oeuvres théologiques et grammaticales de Godescalc d'Orbais*, ed. D. C. Lambot (Louvain: Spicilegium Sacrum Lovaniense, 1945). For Hincmar, see *De Una et Non Trina Deitate* in *Patrologiae cursus completus . . . Series Latina (PL)* ed. J. P. Migne (Paris-Montrose, 1844–1864), 125. For Ratramnus, see *Ratramne de Corbie, Liber de Anima ad Odonem Bellouacensem*, ed. C. D. Lambot in *Analecta Medievalia Namurcensia* 2 (Namur: Centre d'Études Médiévales, 1951). For Eriugena, see *Commentaire sur l'Évangile de Jean*, ed. É. Jeauneau in *Sources Chrétiennes* 180 (Paris: Éditions du Cerf, 1972).

17. These glosses were edited by E. K. Rand who initially and inaccurately attributed them to Eriugena in his doctoral dissertation and later published them

under the title *Johannes Scottus* (München: Beck, 1906). Rand subsequently retracted this thesis. Studies on the issue of the authorship of these glosses and on Eriugena's use of the Boethian tractates are summarized in Mary Brennan, *Guide des études Érigéniennes: Bibliographie commentée des publications 1930–1987* (Paris: Éditions du Cerf, 1989), nos. 27, 98, 174, 176, 186, and 187.

18. Boethius, *De Trinitate* III (Stewart et al., 12–14).

19. Thierry, *Commentum* III.4–11 (Häring, 89–92).

20. Stephen Gersh, "Platonism-Neoplatonism-Aristotelianism: A Twelfth-Century Metaphysical System and Its Sources," in *Renaissance and Renewal in the Twelfth Century*, ed. Robert Benson and Giles Constable (Cambridge, Mass. Harvard University Press, 1982), 512–34 (especially 514–16).

21. For Alan, see *De fide catolica contra haereticos sui temporis* in *PL* 210. For Radulphus, see *In Epistolas et Evangelia Dominicalia Homiliae* in *PL* 155. For the *Summa*, see the edition of J. N. Garvin and J. A. Corbett in *Publications of Medieval Studies* 15 (Notre Dame, Ind.: University of Notre Dame Press, 1958).

22. The notes contained in the translation will indicate instances of unusual citations of *auctores*.

23. *DTr, Introduction* 1–16 (Häring, 65–72). Compare Thierry, *Commentum* II.8–9 (Häring, 70–71).

24. Thierry, *Glosa* II.24 ff (Häring, 273–74).

25. *DTr* II.17 (Häring, 113).

26. *DTr, Introduction* 14 (Häring, 70).

27. *DTr, Prologue* 20–23 (Häring, 82).

28. Boethius, *In Isagogen Porphyrii Commentum Secundum* I.3 in *Corpus Scriptorum Ecclesiasticorum Latinorum* 48 (Vienna: C. Geroldi, 1866–).

29. Thierry, *Lectiones in Boethii librum De Trinitate* II.30 (Häring, 164f).

30. This sentiment is found in Gilbert's comment in his gloss that the text is as useful to theologians as it is to other philosophers: "*tam* usu theologicorum *quam* aliorum philosophorum" (Häring, 192; emphasis added).

31. *DHeb* III.18: "*magis* theologice *quam* secundum aliam facultatem" (Häring, 200, emphasis added).

32. *Magistri Echardi Sermo die b. Augustini Parisius habitus*, ed. Bernhard Geyer in *Meister Eckhart-Die deutschen und lateinischen Werke* V (Stuttgart-Berlin: W. Kohlhammer, 1936), 85–99.

33. "Primo ergo commendatur a pretiositate materiae, id est multitudine sapientiae et scientiae sub diversis habitibus collectae. Ipse enim erat bonus theoricus, egregius logicus et excellentissimus ethicus" (Geyer, 89).

34. Ibid.

35. *DTr, Introductio* 1 (Häring, 65).

36. Geyer, 90–91; compare to *DTr, Introductio* 1–4, 14–15 (Häring, 65–66, 70–71).

Notes to the Letter to Odo

1. Clarembald served as acting master of the Laon school around 1157–1159. The bishop of Laon was Walter of Mortagne (1155–1174), who may have heard of Clarembald through his correspondence with Hugh of St. Victor, one of Clarembald's masters at Paris. We have translated the Latin word *lares* as "abodes." *Lares* were pagan household gods. Clarembald is implying that Aristotle is the pagan titular deity of philosophy. He is thus emphasizing the difference between his academic pursuits and those that the abbot would prefer, as will be seen.

2. The abbot of St. Vincent's at this time was Walter (1156–1174).

3. Calling Boethius a pagan author reveals the strong association of his works solely with the logical works of Aristotle, but the sentiment of Abbot Odo is not unusual. In the *Dialogus de Tribus Quaestionibus,* for example, Othloh of St. Emmeran (1010–1070) laments the fact that the logical works of Boethius are better known than the sacred scriptures (*PL* 146, 60). Clarembald, following his masters, has a different perspective on Boethius and sees him as a true Christian author. As a former student at Chartres, he cannot help but enlighten the abbot about the significance of the theological texts of Boethius.

4. Gilbert of Poitiers died in 1154, before Clarembald composed his gloss. Though a remarkable scholar in his time, he was accused of error in his explanations of the Trinity. His glosses on Boethius's *De Trinitate* were suspect enough to warrant an investigation by a church council in Rheims in 1148 and, as Clarembald reports, were subsequently forbidden to be read or studied either in school or cloister, raising an interesting question concerning the availability of that very text to his confreres.

5. Boethius's father-in-law and companion in intellectual endeavor, the recipient of the *De Trinitate* against the Arians, a heretical sect which arose in the early church under the leadership of Arius. The views of this sect in regard to the Trinity are reviewed by Clarembald in the text. Clarembald finds in the writings of Peter Abelard a neo-Arian strain worthy of forthright condemnation.

6. Odo of Ourscamp, a former student of Abelard and Peter Lombard and in his own right a prominent schoolmaster in Paris in the mid-twelfth century, eventually joined a Cistercian monastery, where he was elected abbot and served in that capacity from 1167–1170, about which time he died.

7. This is the first of several self-referential remarks that Clarembald makes regarding his academic work (cf. *Introductio* 10). It is evident that he considers himself to have been a clever student.

8. Clarembald's understanding of the discipline he calls theology is explained in the body of the gloss and basically follows that of Boethius. Theology is that branch of philosophy that studies those subjects that are completely separated from matter in their own existence and are known by the rational powers of the mind, namely God and the divine ideas which exist in the mind of God. Indeed knowledge

of them can be arrived at only through the supra-rational power of *intellectibilitas*. See the discussions in Clarembald's *Introduction* and in section II of the gloss.

9. This is Clarembald's first of many comments on the proper method necessary to theologize in an orthodox manner in order to avoid error. His contentions against Gilbert and Abelard always include some remark about their failure to observe that proper theological method which Boethius follows in his treatise. The source for these five fallacious methods is apparently Aristotle's *Sophistici Elenchi* I, although there is no direct correspondence between the two texts. It is most interesting to note that Clarembald's use of that Aristotelian text here and in his *Prologue* can be counted among the earliest instances of its citation in the twelfth century. Thierry of Chartres includes the text in his list of critical works in the liberal arts, the *Heptateuchon*, but does not cite it in his glosses on Boethius. It should also be noted that Clarembald draws all his citations of Aristotle from the translations of Boethius (see the collection entitled *Aristotelis Latinus* [Leiden, 1975]).

10. This is the mountain where classical poets were said to sleep in order to be inspired to compose their verse.

11. Stoicism was the major religious and philosophical system from the second century B.C. to the third century C.E. It was founded by Zeno of Citium on the principle that a divine rationality permeated all matter. Matter was composed of the inert and the divine. Thus all things that happen happen in accord with this divine reason. This they called Necessity. Clarembald knew his Stoicism from his reading of Cicero, who was not a Stoic but rather an eclectic Academic.

Notes to Clarembald's Introduction

1. Following his master Thierry, Clarembald combines the Stoic division of philosophy as he finds it in Cicero (speculative, ethical, and logical) with the Aristotelian division of philosophy into theoretical and practical. Clarembald's discussion here and in section II seems to address the concern of the abbot of St. Vincent's regarding the study of secular literature as opposed to the study of sacred scripture.

2. The term *intelligibiliter* is untranslatable, as is the term *intellectibilitas* which occurs later in the text. The terms denote the supra-rational ability of the mind to grasp the nature of disembodied things as they exist in the mind of God. What is unusual here is that Clarembald does not use the adverbial form *intellectualiter* as Boethius does in his text. It is interesting to note that in this passage Clarembald uses the Greek word *idea* rather than the Latin *forma* for "forms" (see also II.59 and II.61). While he most often uses the term *forma* elsewhere, here he may want to underscore the distinction between ideas as they exist in the mind of God and ideas as they are instantiated in created things.

3. Boethius, *De consolatione philosophiae* I p1.

4. Boethius, *De Trinitate* II.

5. Clarembald is commenting on the fact that the Latin word *mathematica* may mean either the science of arithmetic or astrology. *Mathesis* in Greek simply means "the act of learning." Like most twelfth-century scholars, Clarembald was interested in etymologies. The Juvenal quote is from *Saturae* 14.248, *Fourteen Satires of Juvenal,* ed. J. D. Duff (Cambridge: Cambridge University Press, 1914).

6. Clarembald is playing an etymological game with the interplay of the terms *doctrina* and *disciplina,* the former indicating a teacher (*doctor*) and the latter a student (*discipilis*).

7. Clarembald's phrase implies a playful persistence with his teachers. The difference between these two interpretations is that the former (section 9) has an Aristotelian bias insofar as it denies the existence of forms separated from matter. The latter (section 10) offers the Neoplatonic position, which not only assumes the existence of separated forms but holds that they are known inherently by rational beings. This is a clear instance in which Clarembald reveals his Neoplatonism: he affirms his adherence to the views of his masters which are those of the second interpretation. The implication is that the more Aristotelian position is either untenable or at least highly suspect. This nominalist position was held by Peter Abelard, the "bête noire" of this treatise. A passage from the writings of Gilbert of Poitiers, as the following section shows, offers the same nominalist interpretation.

8. The obvious clarity of this citation from Gilbert's *De Trinitate* I.2.10 (Häring, 80) suggests that what Clarembald must be referring to in the phrase *verbis perplexis* ("in an inscrutable passage") is that Gilbert held the Aristotelian position at all.

9. The Latin word *physica* is ultimately derived from the Greek word *phisis* which literally means "growing." As Clarembald says, *natura* is used to translate it. Clarembald's point is that physics deals with natural things. Again we note his interest in etymology.

10. Augustine, *De Trinitate* VII.5, *Corpus Christianorum Series Latina* [CCSL] (Turnholt: Brepols, 1972–), vol. 50.

11. Macrobius, *In Somnium Scipionis Expositio* 1.2.15, ed. Mario Regali (Pisa: Giardini, 1983).

12. These are elements of an *accessus,* a formalized introduction to the material about to be glossed. The *accessus* presents to the reader the basic context of the text and was especially concerned with the purpose and intention of its author. By the time of Clarembald the use of the *accessus* was common practice and he himself composes one for each of his three works.

13. John the Deacon was a contemporary and intellectual companion of Boethius. Two of the *Opuscula Sacra* are addressed to him: one on the Trinity, commonly referred to as *Utrum Pater et Filius* but composed after the *De Trinitate* being glossed here, and one on the mystery of the two natures in one person in Christ, the *Contra Eutychen.* In this latter treatise, Boethius addresses John as his "saintly master and venerable father."

14. Paul, 1 Corinthians 12:3; Cicero, *De deorum natura* 2.66.167, ed. Arthur S. Reese (Cambridge: Cambridge University Press, 1955). Clarembald offers a dramatic closure to his opening comments on the treatise by implying the compatibility of a pagan author to the Christian faith, something which the abbot at St. Vincent's, as reported in the first sentences of the letter to Odo, considered highly suspect.

Notes to Clarembald's Gloss of *De Trinitate*, Prologue

1. A statement which is not extant in the text as we now have it, or based on a faulty recollection of his source. In any event it is not to be found in Seneca.

2. Clarembald's point seems to be the contrast between the detail and attention paid to such trivial matters as bees by Virgil and Seneca as opposed to the somewhat callous and slipshod investigation into the matter of the Holy Trinity by some contemporary theologians, as he goes on to say. A secondary point is the danger of independent investigation which is not submitted to the scrutiny of a competent judge such as Boethius is obviously doing and as Clarembald himself is doing by submitting his manuscript to Odo.

3. We are translating *catholice* as if it were Clarembald's shorthand for the true doctrine of the Roman Catholic Church. His point is that Boethius did not claim to have solved the mystery of the Trinity but only to have discovered a probable solution to a portion of that mystery.

4. Clarembald situates more precisely the question under discussion as a theological question. Since the doctrine on the Trinity is subject to erroneous solutions when it is not carefully resolved by the proper theological method, namely, that method which Boethius uses, Clarembald cautions his readers especially about the intricacies of ambiguous language and the careless use of propositions.

5. See Boethius, *In topicis Ciceronis* I, PL 4.1049A.

6. Ibid., 1.11.

7. Ibid., 1.3.

8. This is an example of Clarembald's Neoplatonic influences. The same thought is found at Gilbert, *De Trinitate* I, *Prologus* 5.

9. Clarembald refers here to ancient Roman theater where an actor would pay a group of people, a "claque," to lead the cheers for him and encourage the audience to approve his performance. Terence often complains about the claque.

10. This refers to the imaginary in the sense of producing images. Thus the "phantasical cell" would be that part of the head in which pictures are produced. This description and that in the following section are taken from Thierry and are typical of the "physical" account of things that was common to the school of Chartres.

11. Saint Augustine in *De Genesi ad litteram* refers to a metaphysical reality, namely the forms of created things as found in the mind of God; see for example II.10–12, *Corpus Scriptorum Ecclesiasticorum Latinorum* (CSEL)(Vienna: C. Geroldi, 1866–), vol. 28. The phrase as used by Boethius, however, denotes more of an epistemological relationship between the mind of God and the rational soul.

Notes to Section I

1. Cicero, *De deorum natura* II.28.72. This is a "folk etymology" drawn from the fact that *superstitio* and *superstito* both resemble *supersto* which means "to survive."

2. *Religandus* means respect for what is sacred whereas *relegendo* means to read something over again.

3. Clarembald is here distinguishing between faith, which is the doctrinal content, and religion, which is the cultic expression, of the Christian. Hence deviation from faith is called heresy; deviation from cult is called superstition.

4. The Athanasian Hymn, or as it is commonly called the Athanasian Creed and known by its *incipit, Quicumque,* was not composed by St. Athanasius (295–373), but is considered a later work, perhaps of the sixth century. It is associated with Athanasius because of its strong emphasis on the Trinity and the Incarnation. It was recited after the homily during Sunday Masses.

5. James 2:19.

6. So it is for Clarembald that the demons are not saved because they lack that devotion (religion) by which the content of the faith is brought into practice and loved.

7. Hebrews 11:1.

8. This passage portends the Trinitarian themes of the text: three which are distinct yet one.

9. Clarembald has now distinguished three nominal senses of the term "faith." The first, presented in section 4, is simple belief as opposed to cultic practices. The second sense, found in section 5, is saving faith by which a believer is redeemed. The third, offered here in section 6, is doctrinal faith which sets forth the truths of the Christian religion. As the second and third are virtues in Clarembald's schema, they denote respectively union with God and union with the Catholic church.

10. Thierry, *Commentum* I.3 (Häring, 63).

11. Psalm 19:5.

12. Romans 10:12. This explanation of faith as a Neoplatonic universal is intriguing.

13. Perhaps underlying the Latin word *sententia* is the Greek word *idea,* which Clarembald uses elsewhere for "form."

14. This well-known definition of person is from the fifth of the Boethian theological tractates, *Contra Eutychen et Nestorium* III, a definition which Boethius introduces there in his argument for the Catholic understanding of the two natures in one person in Christ. Clarembald will return to this definition in V.13 below.

15. See *Prologue* 13.

16. What follows is a rather standard discussion of species that depends on material found in Thierry's *Commentum* I. Clarembald's purpose here is unclear, as he will break off this discussion rather abruptly at 19. He appears to be conversant in the arguments that he reviews and his position is clear, that humanity and man are

not species in the same way. Is there a veiled reference to Gilbert of Poitiers and Abelard in 13 (*famosi doctores*) regarding the nature of species, in anticipation of Clarembald's later overt attack on Gilbert's trinitarian theology beginning in 24? Is this later attack the "something else" mentioned in 19 as the reason for leaving this discussion and returning to his gloss on the text?

17. Mathematics here is presented as abstractive while reason proceeds as descriptive.

18. For Boethius's concept of these "common conceptions of the mind" or axioms, see his *De Hebdomadibus*. Clarembald discusses these in section III of his gloss on that treatise.

19. Here again Clarembald highlights the necessity of rejecting arguments from natural analogy and adhering to the Boethian method of argumentation based on reasoning according to the power of *intellectibilitas* (see Introduction, pp. xxii–xxiv, and Clarembald's *Introduction* 4).

20. Gilbert, *De Trinitate* I.12–13 (Häring, 72–73).

21. Clarembald expresses a deference here in regard to the famous Gilbert, but a deference that is guarded and that distances Clarembald from Gilbert. Clarembald will repeat this position more than once to make sure it is clear that he is not aligning himself with Gilbert despite his familiarity with the bishop's ideas; see for example III.36.

22. John 14:28.

23. This passage combines the Neoplatonic notion of all things flowing from the one with the Aristotelian categories of substance, quality, quantity, etc.

24. Boethius, *De institutione arithmetica* I.3, ed. Godofredus Friedlein (Frankfurt: Minerva, 1966).

25. It is not exactly clear why Clarembald thinks it important to bring this matter up. But perhaps he is issuing a veiled warning to those who stray from the orthodox Catholic position. Or perhaps since he has just cited a condemned author he wants to reassert his own orthodoxy by his recounting of Arius's fate in which he enthusiastically concurs.

26. Sedulius, *Carmen Paschali* I.303, PL 19,585A.

27. This refers to Abelard's classifications of the Father as genus and the Son as species which Clarembald raises in his *Prologue* 2.

28. Although Clarembald claims to have read Abelard, his citations are all taken from Bernard's letter to Pope Innocent (*Epistola* 190) in which the abbot denounces and derides Abelard, who was ultimately condemned at the Council of Sens in 1140.

29. *Stulilogia* can be rendered "systematic stupidity."

30. Clarembald is pointing out the confusion of Abelard's statement which arises from a lack of clarity in determining whether the copula is to be taken grammatically or existentially.

31. This conflict between theology and logic in the liberal arts anticipates the serious debate at the University of Paris in the next century in which St. Thomas Aquinas would argue strongly against Siger of Brabant, Boethius of Dacia, and

others for holding to a "two truth" theory: that is, that one truth is found in the arts, notably in Aristotle, and another truth is found in Christian revelation.

32. Clarembald is charging Abelard with a logical inconsistency in assigning to the genus specific powers which the genus would not have. He seems to think that Abelard's problem is that in using the analogy of genus to species to describe the relationship between the Father and Son he has drifted from a logical relationship to a real one.

33. Clarembald is maintaining here the distinction between things as they are in reality and things as they are known, a distinction which he clearly implies the heretics as well as such figures as the bishop of Poitiers have either failed to recognize or simply ignored.

34. The manuscripts here have several readings: "sed simul ex," "sed simul et," and "sed simul et ex." These reveal some anxiety of the copyists with Clarembald's meaning. In any case the sense is clear, namely that a strong contrast between the real and the logical is being upheld.

35. Clarembald here is making a pointed joke which has a twofold interpretation, that man can be counted among asses in the sense either of the genus animal or of stupidity. While the context would indicate the latter, Clarembald has certainly allowed for equivocation here and underscores his general point that words have multiple meanings and those need to be treated with great care and respect especially in conveying theological doctrine.

36. Aristotle, *De topicis* I.5, *Aristoteles Latinus,* ed. L. Minio-Paluello (Leiden: E. J. Brill, 1969).

Notes to Section II

1. Clarembald embeds the phrase "by the intellect" into his citation of Boethius. This is a common strategy of his commentary in order to highlight the point he wants to make.

2. Plato, *Timaeus* 44E, *Timaeus, Critias, Cleitophon, Menexenus, Epistles,* trans. R. G. Bury (Cambridge, Mass.: Harvard University Press, 1981). Clarembald borrows this citation from Thierry in *Commentum* II.1.

3. Clarembald re-presents here the comments he made in his *Introduction* regarding the divisions of philosophy according to the instruments of knowledge possessed by the mind.

4. It is not clear here whether the phrase *praedicta instrumenta grossa* is referring to the last three senses (touch, taste, and smell), thus establishing a hierarchy of the senses, or to all five senses, thus establishing the inferiority of sense knowledge to imaginative and rational knowledge, or both.

5. Clarembald is here playing on the etymology of *imaginatio* which is from *imago*, which means a picture or a likeness.

6. Note here the relationship of *imago* to phantasm: both refer to the physicality of the object as it is known according to the proper instrument of the mind. Clarembald is laying the foundation for the non-physical nature of theological objects that can be known by the mind only according to the supra-rational power of *intellectibilitas,* which lacks any physical instrument.

7. Plato, *Timaeus* 51E.

8. Clarembald here uses the accusative infinitive construction for his indirect discourse rather than a *quia* clause which is his wont. He is trying to show his classical learning.

9. Genesis 1:2. In his *Tractatulus,* Clarembald offers an extended "physical" commentary on the six days of creation, in imitation of Thierry's *De Sex Dierum Operibus.* He follows a similar line of thought in his scriptural exegesis here.

10. Ovid, *Metamorphoses* 2.541, ed. W. S. Anderson (Stuttgart-Leipzig: B. G. Teubner, 1991).

11. Clarembald is here being very careful to distinguish between separating (*sequestrare*) and abstracting (*abstrahere*). What is not separable in nature may indeed be abstracted by reason, but what is abstracted by reason is not necessarily separable in nature.

12. Boethius, *De institutione arithmetica* I.1.

13. The use of the term *speculato* (translated here as "investigated") indicates that Clarembald is speaking of something that is beyond the power of the mind to grasp, and thus reflects that *intellectibilitas* by which divine things can in some way be known by the mind.

14. The word in this sentence is adverbial, *intellectibiliter,* but the translation renders it as a noun to retain its terminological weight: the noun form of the word will be used throughout the translation.

15. Clarembald is proffering here an epistemological hierarchy, wherein physics would take the lowest position because it is least demanding on the intellect since its object can be perceived by senses and studied by experimentation. Mathematics, on the other hand, demands a heightened rational ability insofar as its object is abstract from matter and must be considered in the mind alone, even though that object is admitted to exist only in conjunction with matter. Theology, as will be seen, holds the highest position not only because its object is completely separate from matter but also because it proceeds according to the supra-rational power of *intellectibilitas.* All of this is dependent upon the concept of the physiology of thought, as discussed earlier in this book (II.4–8).

16. Cicero, *De deorum natura* I.18.46.

17. Clarembald is asserting that there are three forms. First there is the perfect form, which is God. Then there are the forms of all created things which exist in the mind of God and these are described as "images." Finally there are the forms which actually inhere in matter to produce the created things. Physics and mathematics, each according to its own proper method, can only consider the forms in this last category. Theology alone by the power of *intellectibilitas* is capable of considering the

first two forms. Form is the "perfection and equality" of a thing in that without form a thing could not be exactly the kind of thing it is, as the following section explains.

18. It is thus natural for man to want and to be able to know God through the power of *intellectibilitas*. This derives from Genesis 1–2, wherein man is described as being created in the image and likeness of God.

19. Exodus 3:14.

20. Note the use of the Greek, which means "according to stuff." Later in the text at 41 Clarembald or his scribe mistakenly writes *kaka* for *kata*.

21. Thierry, *Commentum* II.18ff. (Häring, 74–75).

22. See I.19–42.

23. Aristotle, *Physics* 191a7–12, *The Basic Works of Aristotle*, ed. Richard McKeon (New York: Random House, 1941).

24. See II.22.

25. See the discussion in II.33.

26. Aristotle, *Liber Perihermenias PL* 64.265.

27. Thierry, *Commentum* II.30–31 is being quoted here and in several of the following passages, as indicated by the punctuation. It is interesting to note that while Clarembald seeks to specify his citations, especially from those with whom he disagrees, such as Gilbert of Poitiers, he does not indicate his direct citation of Thierry here.

28. See II.21.

29. *Consimiliar et officialia* literally means "similar and dutiful things," but William of Conches (*De philosophia mundi* I.21, *PL* 172) gives the sense of the terminology when he writes "dutiful things, like hands and feet. . . ."

30. Again citations from Thierry, *Commentum* II.33 and 34 (Häring, 78–79).

31. A perfect square has equality of length of sides and equality of angles.

32. This material is taken from Thierry, *Commentum* II.34 (Häring, 78–79). The point here is that the Son is the equal of the Father because the Father, who is described as "unity (one) at once (eternal)," in generating the Son generates what is equal to himself. Thus the Son is the "equality of unity," and is in all respects equal to the Father save in this alone, that the Father generates and the Son is generated. This description is further evidence which Clarembald wishes to utilize to prove the unity of substance and distinction of persons in the Trinity.

33. The argument here is from the opposite, namely since what destroys is odious, therefore what unites must be loved.

34. Thierry, *Commentum* II.37 (Häring, 80).

35. Clarembald does not explain Thierry's surprising and unexplained introduction of the phrase "aequalitas essendi" for the now familiar "aequalites unitatis" in describing the Son in this sentence. The meaning of the two phrases is identical since being and unity are the same for Clarembald.

36. See II.24, where Clarembald began this discussion of the Trinity of persons.

37. This again is a quote from Thierry (*Commentum* II.42), who has substituted *integritas* for the Boethian term *aequalitas*. The sense is the same.

38. See note 20 above.

39. See II.26–30.

40. Clarembald is particularly fond of this statement and repeats or rephrases it in *Tractatulus* 23 and *De Hebdomadibus* III.19 and IV.30.

41. Martianus Felix Capella, *Liber Nuptiis philologiae et mercurii* I.64, ed. James Willis (Leipzig: B. G. Teubner, 1983).

42. Ibid., II.206.

43. Gilbert, *De Trinitate* I.3.16 (Häring, 105).

44. This refers to the second of the false teaching methods which Clarembald introduces in his *Letter to Odo* 7. The reference is to Gilbert's *De Trinitate* I.3.6 (Häring, 102).

45. Terence, *Andria* 17, ed. Richard C. Monti (Bryn Mawr, Penn.: Thomas Library, Bryn Mawr College, 1986).

46. Aristotle, *De topicis* I.11. Clarembald again is cautious in his criticism of Gilbert. Here he is saying that Gilbert, described as *magister*, may be seen to confuse the issue because he is approaching it in an overly philosophical manner and thus earning for his position the somewhat derogatory title of *positio* which in Aristotle's understanding is an unusual and somewhat mystifying supposition, such as Anthisthenes' view that contradictions are impossible.

47. The term translated here as "matter" is *silva*, which is literally "woods," a direct translation of the Greek *hyle*. Clarembald is critiquing Gilbert's use of terms or more correctly the direction from which he takes his terms. For Clarembald things are called by the term "form" on account of their relation to the prime form. Gilbert, in Clarembald's reading, applies the term from the characteristics of material things. This is another example of what is becoming a standard charge, that Gilbert confuses the particular with the universal. Clarembald is also very defensive of the traditional Platonic metaphysics, while Gilbert could be seen as exploring a more Aristotelian metaphysics and all of its consequences.

48. Boethius, *De consolatione philosophiae* V.6.

49. See II.51–55.

50. Clarembald does not give an example here, probably presuming that the reader takes his meaning without it.

Notes to Section III

1. Two comments need to be made here regarding the translation of what follows. The first is that the Latin word *unitas* is translated variously as "unit" or "unity," as the context demands a reference to a single thing or to that which makes a thing

singular. The second is that in describing the Trinity, Clarembald will sometimes use a collective noun with a singular form of the verb to emphasize the orthodox "three persons in one nature" doctrine which Boethius is explaining.

2. See I.5.

3. It is interesting to note that Clarembald uses the Latin title above and the Greek title here.

4. By inferior Clarembald is speaking logically, in that what species is below or inferior to genus.

5. Once again Clarembald is affirming the distinction between what is logical (the number by which we count things) and what is real (the number which inheres in things).

6. Clarembald, following Thierry, reverses the explanation of Boethius regarding the two kinds of number. Boethius holds that the number by which we count leads to plurality, but the number which is in things does not. Clarembald clearly states this Boethian position, but follows Thierry's number theory in holding that it is the number which is in things which leads to plurality, for the number by which we count does not lead to plurality. The reason for this divergence is that Boethius was following the number theory set forth in Aristotle's *Physics,* a text unknown in the twelfth century. The two Chartrians are following the view of pseudo-Augustinian *De musica* as cited in the text. Cf. Gersh, "Platonism-Neoplatonism-Aristotelianism," 512–36.

7. Pseudo-Augustibe, *De musica* VI.2.2, *PL* 32.

8. The distinction here is between "repeating" and "adding." The former does not produce a plurality despite the repetition of the unit; the latter does.

9. Aristotle, *De categoria, PL* 64. 181D.

10. Boethius, *De consolatione philosophiae* V.4.

11. Boethius, *De institutione arithmetica* I.3. The Latin terms here are *aequalitas* and *inaequalitas.* Clarembald is understandably unaware of the twofold distinction of number which Aristotle does make in *Physics* I.

12. Pseudo-Augustine, *Categoriae decem* 10, *Aristotles Latinus,* ed. L. Minio-Paluello (Bruges-Paris: Desclée de Brouwer, 1961).

13. Pseudo-Augustine, *De musica* VI.2.2.

14. Clarembald is clearly working from memory (or lack thereof) here, but why this is the case is another question. Perhaps he is composing this section somewhere where he did not have access to the primary texts or perhaps it is an affected style similar to other comments he makes throughout the text. Perhaps, though, Clarembald recognizes that the two distinctions of number (Boethius and Augustine) do not in fact agree, but is not willing to reject the discussion of his revered master Thierry upon which he is basing his gloss.

15. Clarembald in the following passage will pun on the Latin words for "synonym" and "univocal." In Latin synonym is *multivocus* (many words), univocal is *univocus* (one word). The examples are for synonym, the sword, the brand, and the blade; for the univocal, sun, sun, and sun.

16. See III.7.

17. Clarembald is here demonstrating exactly what he claims the five erroneous forms of teaching do—see preface 6–10. Also check his remarks on Abelard and Gilbert regarding careful use of language.

18. Sedulius, *Carmen Paschali* I.319f. The meaning is also metrically underscored. He is also punning on the multiple meanings of *summus*.

19. Clarembald is referring to Gilbert's discussion in *De Trinitate* I.3.32ff (Häring, 108ff) which Clarembald finds confusing in this matter. Clarembald feels justified in his confusion for even the Rheims Council in 1148 found the entire text sufficiently unclear to condemn it.

20. The first quote is from the Boethian text. The second is from Thierry's *Commentum* IV.1 (Häring, 95).

Notes to Section IV

1. Clarembald's point is that there is here a violation of the rules of grammar, for the first phrase denotes something attributive or accidental but the second something predicative. Note that from the beginning of III Clarembald has rejected the nominalist position regarding predicates and upholds the realist position of the school of Chartres.

2. Pseudo-Augustine, *Categoriae decem* 3. The text is attributed to Augustine by Clarembald, but its authorship is unknown. Clarembald is arguing that while Augustine borrowed from the text of Aristotle, he did not adhere to Aristotle's position regarding the predicates.

3. Ibid.

4. Cicero, *Topica* VII.31.

5. Pseudo-Augustine, *Categoriae decem* 3. Note the difference here: Cicero understood "impressa" literally but Augustine takes it figuratively.

6. Even though Clarembald claimed in his letter to Odo that he studied the *De Trinitate* under Hugh, there is no extant manuscript of such a gloss. It could be that there was such a gloss and it is now lost, or that Hugh only lectured on this treatise. It appears to us that Clarembald is citing Hugh from memory. This is in fact the only time that Hugh is cited in Clarembald's gloss.

7. Pseudo-Augustine, *Categoriae decem* 3.

8. Having set forth the notion of a predicate which he wants to be operative in this discussion, Clarembald now presents his understanding of the non-applicability of the predicates to the Deity (sections 14–39). After that he will resume his gloss of the Boethian text.

9. Psalm 136. This is one of the very infrequent references to Scripture and is the only one which uses Scripture as proof for the assertions made rather than to reinforce an otherwise proved position.

10. Augustine, *De diversis quaestionibus* 83.20, CCSL 44A.

11. Euclid, *Elementa* I, ed. E. S. Stamatis (Leipzig: Teubner, 1969).

12. Clarembald's citation here from Euclid is unique to his gloss and not borrowed from Thierry.

13. Wisdom 11:21.

14. This appears to be the source for what Clarembald describes as the five false methods of teaching which he presents in the *Letter to Odo*.

15. This presentation foreshadows the argument of the *De Hebdomadibus* gloss.

16. The "adversary" of sections 20–28, who is now described as lying "miserably and impiously," is most likely the Cathars who held that God did not create the physical world which is inherently evil.

17. Psalm 13.1.

18. See II.23.

19. Pseudo-Augustine, *Categoriae decem* 16.

20. Literally, "nothing is had which has a haver." The problem is that the Latin word for "state" or "condition" is *habere*, which also means "to have" as "to possess."

21. Boethius, *In librum Aristotelis Peri hermenias* II.10, *Aristoteles Latinus*, ed. L. Minio-Paluello (Bruges-Paris: Desclée de Brouwer, 1961).

22. See *Prologue* 22 and II.8.

23. This is taken from Thierry's *Commentum* IV.16 (Häring, 99). Thierry has taken it from Pseudo-Augustine, *Categoriae decem* 1.

24. Häring unaccountably diverges from the reading of all three manuscripts by omitting the "non" in the last clause of this sentence, which should read "quae non sunt homo." Perhaps he does this because of Clarembald's later omission of the "non" in repeating the clause in section 59; but there Clarembald explains the textual variant he has introduced.

25. See II.48–49.

26. Boethius, *In Topica Ciceronis* III, *PL* 64.

27. Pseudo-Augustine, *Categoriae decem* 12.

28. The division of time is threefold: eternity, sempiternity, and now. The first is applied to the Deity, the second to eternally existing natural things, such as the heavenly spheres, and the third to man and other creatures.

29. Clarembald has mistakenly taken the Boethian phrase "quod est nunc" to be a relative clause explaining the *nomen* at the beginning of the sentence, rather than being a temporal phrase meaning simply "the present," as this translation understands it. Boethius is speaking in the passage about the etymology of the term 'sempiternity' and derives it from *semper* and *aeternitas*. Clarembald however focuses on the term *nunc* and even omits the term *aeternitas* in his gloss. His explication is impossible unless he intends that *nunc* and *aeternitas* mean the same thing.

30. Genesis 4:17f

31. Cicero, *De inventione* 1.26.39–40, trans. H. M. Hubbell (Cambridge, Mass.: Harvard University Press, 1968).

32. Cicero, *De inventione* 1.26.38.

33. Cicero, *De inventione* 1.26.37. It is interesting to note that Clarembald reverses the three examples as they appear in Cicero.

Notes to Section V

1. This is again a reference to Clarembald's concern for proper teaching methods, as mentioned in the *Letter to Odo*.

2. This is the Council of Nicea which defined the Trinity as "one God in three persons."

3. The Greek word *hypostasis* means "substantial nature." The problem is that the Latin *persona* does not quite translate it.

4. See I.8–9.

5. The *per se notum* or self-evident axiom will be defined and discussed more extensively in *De Hebdomadibus* III.

Notes to Section VI

1. Clarembald may be showing off a bit by using names drawn from the plays of Terence, thus demonstrating his classical erudition. See note 45 of section II.

2. *Introduction* 7 (Häring, 68).

3. Hebrews 11:1.

Notes to Clarembald's Gloss of De Hebdomadibus

1. Aristotle, *Topicis* I.1.

2. Ibid.

3. Aristotle, *Analytica Priora* 4, *Aristoteles Latinus,* ed. L. Minio-Paluello (Bruges-Paris: Desclée de Brouwer, 1975).

4. See the comments on this term in our Introduction (pp. xxii–xxiv) and in II.8ff. Clarembald, unlike Thierry, introduces the term into this discussion to reinforce his view that the treatise is theological in nature, as will become clear in what follows.

5. Clarembald presents his *accessus* here and in II.6.

6. Augustine, *De Doctrina Christiana* II.6.7.

7. Macrobius, *Commentum in Somnium Scipionis* I.2.19–20. The goddesses are Demeter and Persephone.

8. Galen was a Greek physician whose medical texts were available in Latin translation to Clarembald at Chartres. Clarembald makes reference to two Galen texts: here the *Tegni* and later in section 15 the *Ex Hippocrate*. It is noteworthy that Thierry never cites Galen in his Boethian glosses. Clarembald is clearly incorporating into this text some insights from his own studies. Clarembald's point in raising the issue of teaching methods has to do with establishing the proper method to be used in solving the question. This is a theological question, not a question for the arts, and thus must not drift into a method more suited to the arts. As will be made clear in succeeding notes, Clarembald is here preparing the grounds for his refutation of Gilbert of Poitiers's reading of the text.

9. Unlike the *De Trinitate* gloss, Clarembald's citations of the Boethian text are much more interspersed with his own words and phrases as if a paraphrase. He offers no explanation for this change in mode of citation.

10. *DTr, Prologue* 5. This is the first of several references to the *De Trinitate* gloss. Clarembald presumes that his reader is familiar with that text.

11. The term here is *existentia* and is an abstraction. The three levels of being therefore exist in the mind of God, in matter such that they can be named, and as actually existing sensible things.

12. Clarembald is distinguishing here between the way a thing exists and the way a thing is known.

13. Priscian, *Institutiones* I.1.1, *Prisciani Caesariensis Grammatici Opera*, ed. Augustus Krehl (Leipzig: In Libraria Weidmannia, 1819–1820). Priscian was a sixth-century A.D. grammarian who taught in Constantinople. His *Institutiones Grammaticae* was the standard grammatical text throughout the Middle Ages.

14. Cicero, *De topicis* V.27.

15. Pseudo-Augustine, *Categoriae decem* 5.

16. Pythagoras was a sixth-century B.C. philosopher from Sicily.

17. Boethius, *De institutione arithmetica* I.1.

18. The point here is that the purpose of the hebdomads is to guide the mind to the truth. Any principle known by the mind, if the mind uses it properly according to the different sciences to which that principle can belong, will assist the mind in discerning the truth. The examples Clarembald offers in the paragraph illustrate this point. It is not known why Clarembald omits another rather obvious meaning, seven or week, designating a weekly gathering of Boethius and his friends to discuss philosophical and theological matters.

19. Since Being Itself is beyond comprehension, it cannot be the genus of a substance for insofar as a substance is known, its genus is known.

20. According to this interpretation, the question is problematic because of the difficulty in determining the genus of substances in logical categories. Häring has tried to highlight this difficulty by inserting commas in the text thusly: "substantiae in eo, quod sunt, bonae sint."

This interpretation appears to be that of Gilbert of Poitiers as found in his gloss on this *opusculum* at I.110ff (Häring, 211ff). Clarembald would charge generally that Gilbert wrongly approaches the treatise as logical rather than as metaphysical and more specifically here that Gilbert twists the Boethian formula out of its natural grammatical sense (the *quod* ought to be understood as a conjunction, not as a pronoun).

Clarembald will dispute Gilbert's interpretation in other places in this treatise, although he never refers to his antagonist by name as he does in the *De Trinitate* gloss.

21. Matthew 7:6.

22. Clarembald is reading into this short line a significant amount of the subsequent argument.

23. John 21:6.

24. In this passage the *a* has the force of "on account of" rather than "by," as is explained in the following section. The difference is that in the former case the trivial nature of the vulgar keeps them from focusing their minds on difficult issues because such issues are not a source of merriment. In the latter case, however, the vulgar approach the serious issues precisely in order to make fun of them. Thus in the first instance the vulgar are simply weak; in the second they are malicious.

25. Aristotle, *Praedicamenta*, PL LXIV.159A–163B.

26. Aristotle, *Analytica Priora* I.4-21.

27. The source for this information is Galen's *Ex Hippocrate* I.4–5.

28. The purpose of this passage is to stress most clearly the requirement of a common conception of the mind that it be understood immediately upon being heard. If a statement has to be thought about in order to be grasped, then either it does not fall under the definition of a *conceptio* or the hearer is not perspicacious enough to grasp it.

29. Pseudo-Augustine, *Categoriae decem* 10.

30. Epicurus (341–270 B.C.) accepted the atomic theory of Democritus. This view and other fundamentals of Epicurianism were set forth by Lucretius in 54 B.C. in *De natura rerum*.

31. In emphasizing the theological nature of the treatise, Clarembald is taking exception to the position of Gilbert of Poitiers who argues that the text can be as useful to philosophers as to theologians (*tam usu theologicorum quam aliorum philosophorum*), and prefers to read the treatise as dealing with the existence of natural things (thus *esse* is not God, but simply existing). See his gloss on *De Hebdomadibus*, especially I.34.

32. Romans 11:36.

33. *De Celestis Hierarchia* 2, ed. J.-P. Migne, *Patrologiae cursus completus . . . Series graeca* (Paris-Montrouge, 1857–1866), vol 3. The Greek writings of this sixth-century anonymous author known as pseudo-Dionysius were known in the west through the translations of the ninth-century theologian Johannes Scotus Eriugena.

34. John 1:3.

35. For Clarembald's discussion on the four modes of necessity, see *DTr* II.43–47.

36. This axiom is described as being set out *dissonanter.* The point is that the preceding four axioms flow out from one another in a logical sequence. This fifth axiom, however, marks another starting point.

37. The reference is found in *Johannes Scottus* 52 (ed. E. K. Rand). Remigius of Auxerre was thought to have composed what are considered to be the earliest glosses on all of the Boethian theological tractates in the ninth century. Later research has shown this to be false and thus has entitled these anonymous glosses as simply *The Auxerre Commentary.*

38. See II.7

39. Plato, *Timaeus* 272. Calcidius lived in the late fourth century and was probably a Christian. His commentary on Plato's *Timaeus* had significant influence in the twelfth century and especially at the school of Chartres. See chapter 6 of Stephen Gersh's *Middle Platonism and Neoplatonism—The Latin Tradition,* vol. II (Notre Dame, Ind.: University of Notre Dame Press, 1986).

40. For simplicity is the furthest thing from the compound existence from which it is differentiated in this passage.

41. Martianus Felix Capella, *De Nuptiis philologiae et mercurii* I.1.

42. This episode is taken from *De Ordine Creatuarum Liber* 6.3, PL 83 The text, though attributed to the seventh-century etymologist Isidore of Seville, has been traced to Ireland.

43. See I.5

44. Boethius, *De Consolatione philosophiae* IIIp10.

45. Ibid., III.18.

46. See V.42

47. Galen, *Ars medica* 17, ed. K. G. Kuhn, *Medicorum Graecorum opera* I (Leipzig, 1821).

48. See II.7

49. *DTr* VI.11–12

50. This is an improvisation on Clarembald's part, for Boethius does not list this as one of the axioms for the solution of the question.

51. See IV.28.

52. Boethius, *De institutione arithmetica* II.30.

53. The reference is to *De Trinitate* II,13.

54. See IV.28.

55. The identity of Rutenus is unknown.

56. Boethius, *De consolatione philosophiae* III.9.

57. Genesis 1:1.

58. Psalm 32:9.

59. Plato, *Timaeus* 30C.

60. Genesis 1:32.

61. This line of discussion does not arise in the Boethian text nor does Clarembald's principle source, Thierry, present it. The discussion is essentially Augustinian;

see for example Augustine's comments in *De Genesi ad litteram* IV.3–6, *CSEL* 28, and *De ordine* I.1.1, *CSEL* 63.

62. Plato, *Timaeus* 28A.

63. Boethius, *De consolatione philosophiae* IV.6.

64. Thierry, *Commentum super Ebdomadas Boetii* 105–107 (Häring, 423–24).

DAVID B. GEORGE
is professor and chair of classics at Saint Anselm College.

JOHN R. FORTIN, O.S.B.,
is a Benedictine monk of Saint Anselm Abbey in Manchester, New Hampshire, an associate professor of philosophy at Saint Anselm College, and director of the Institute for Saint Anselm Studies.